AFRODISIA

Also by Ted Joans

A Black Pow-Wow of Jazz Poems

A Black Manifesto in Jazz Poetry and Prose

AFRODISIA

New Poems by Ted Joans

Marion Boyars   London

A MARION BOYARS BOOK
Distributed by
Calder & Boyars Ltd
18 Brewer Street, London W1R 4AS

First published in Great Britain in 1976 by
Marion Boyars Publishers Ltd
18 Brewer Street, London W1R 4AS

Originally published in the United States of America
by Hill & Wang

© Ted Joans 1970

ALL RIGHTS RESERVED

ISBN 0 7145 2507 3 Cased Edition
ISBN 0 7145 2524 3 Paperback Edition

Any paperback edition of this book whether published simultaneously
with, or subsequent to, the cased edition is sold subject to the
condition that it shall not, by way of trade, be lent, resold, hired
out, or otherwise disposed of, without the publishers' consent,
in any form of binding or cover other than that in which it is
published.

No part of this publication may be reproduced, stored in a retrieval
system, or transmitted, in any form or by any means, electronic,
mechanical, photocopying, recording or otherwise, except brief
extracts for the purposes of review, without the prior written
permission of the copyright owner and publisher.

Printed and bound in Great Britain by
REDWOOD BURN LIMITED
Trowbridge & Esher

TO THE BLACK SISTERS, YELLOW, RED, AND BROWN,
AND TOO THE WHITE ONES THAT AFRODISIA FOUND,
and to my MOTHER
do I dedicate this volume of poems

CONTENTS

Africa   *1*
Africa   *3*
Afrique Accidentale   *4*
Ouagadougou Ouagadougou   *9*
Tide of March   *10*
Palm Tree   *11*
Illustration   *12*
A Black First   *13*
You'd Better Watch Out   *13*
Ghorfas   *14*
C_____ C_____ Raiders   *15*
Cinque Maggio   *16*
Bane Black   *18*
Zoo You Too!   *19*
Happy Fool Year!!   *19*
Home   *20*
The Boat Ride   *21*
Wild West Savages   *22*
The Reward   *24*
Lets Do Something   *24*
Way Down Yonder   *25*
Up Out of the African   *26*
The Protective Grigri   *27*
We All Is   *27*
Directions   *28*
The Click Chick   *29*
Okay, You Are Afraid of Africa   *30*
The African Ocean   *31*
Illustration   *32*
Illustration   *33*
Illustration   *33*
Illustration   *34*
Illustration   *35*
Illustration   *36*
Black Mane   *37*

The Night of the Shark   38
Illustration   41
Dutch Treatment   42
Still Traveling   44
Buy and Buy   46
Le Fou de Bamba   48
The Black Cowerie   49
Belief Brings Relief   50
As Don Took Off at Dawn   51
Sand   56
Louvre Afrique   57
I'm ?????   58
Illustration   59
Tangerine Scene   60
Harlem to Picasso   61
All White on Europe Sixty-Nine Western Front   62
Black Repeater   63
My Trip   64

      Erotica   69
Afrodisia   71
Cuntinent   72
Unsalvageable   78
God Blame America!!   79
Bed   80
The Sink   81
Big   82
Knee Deep   85
Love   86
Round   87
Interview   88
Why Cry   89
Illustration   90
Meating   92
My Love   93

Love Way   95
Ah-So!   95
Painter   96
One Blue Note   97
Promenade du Venus   98
Twenty-Three Is Next   99
Dear Miss America   100
My Beauty Wades   102
Journey   103
Sure Really   104
The Source   105
The Passing Couple   106
All in One   107
Advice Alphabeticamerica   108
Yes Indeed Blues   114
Raining Blues   114
White Lace   115
Chickitten Gitten!   116
Postalove Blues   117
Love Tight   118
The Flirt   119
Sweet Potato Pie   120
Joansizeven   121
The Hump   122
Check Up Blues   123
Magic Pants   124
The Underground Bitch   125
Jazz Anatomy   131
Mouth   132
Cool   133
125 Ways to Sex or Sexplosion   136
It Is Ours   137
Pubik Pak   138
Dont Let the Minute Spoil the Hour   141
Later!   142
Illustration   144

Cold Petroleum 147
Oversea Sister 148
Kidsnatchers 149
Are You Too, Able? 149
I Am the Lover 150

AFRICA

AFRICA

Africa   I guard your memory
Africa   you are in me
My future is your future
Your wounds are my wounds
The funky blues I cook
  are black like you—Africa
Africa   my motherland
America is my fatherland
although I did not choose it to be
Africa   you alone can make me free
Africa   where the rhinos roam
Where I learned to swing
before America became my home
Not like a monkey but in my soul
Africa   you are the rich with natural gold
Africa   I live and study for thee
And through you I shall be free
Someday I'll come back and see
Land of my mothers, where a black god made me
My Africa, your Africa, a free continent to be

AFRIQUE ACCIDENTALE

To Hoyt Fuller

back on the boat, now bound for Afrique, I float
land in Dakar, destination Timbuctu, not so very far
Dakar/Niger chemin de fer, Tombouctou, très loin from here
Thies, Diourbel, Kaffrine and sad Tambacounda
there's a sign to remember, "Vive Notre Frère Lumumba!"
show aint no Chattanooga Choo Choo
passengers wearing grigris and Western voodoo
Wow! a cheetah chasing the giraffe
going faster than this train, now aint that a laff?
customs here in Senegal Kidira
staying in Kayes Mali tonight, Timbuctu is nearer
fastass cheetahs usually chase gazelles
ah ha! theres a skin for sell
market place jumpin
guess I'll buy sumpin
Hello, little blackdoll can I be your man?
Oh no? You know I'm a jiving Afroamerican
Gotta ketch dis train rite-a-way
passing through the town of Bafoulabé
Fangala, Toukete, Baulouli and Kita
Timbuctu, How far, How far?
It's hot in this train & everybody sweats with me
vultures up there something must be dead, yep phew wee!
road sign reads, "Gue en saison seche"
also limonade, and fried African peche
Wow! my first hot April scene
ant hills, giants that pick you clean
Negala, Kati . . . and now Bamako
accommodations? in the capital? why no!
Russians, Chinese Reds, and some Poles
Karl Marx sent 'em here, sun bakes their souls
air-conditioned U.S. Embassy

The big white country being "real nice" to me?
visit chamber of commerce for map
buying African art, but no tourist crap
studying map with Frenchman laying out our plans
he's the guide and chauffeur, works for Trans Africane
week in Bamako, up the river by canoe and motor pirogue we go
women washing bright clothes
my how their nude bodies glows
River Niger like the Mississippi
dig that broad, show is hippy!
Koulikore first stop changing to paddlewheel slow and hot
sleep on the riverboat, just like U.S.A. South
just mosquitoes biting everywhere, even inside my mouth
roasted goat with French imported cuisine
I'm going to Tombouctou, Je suis king & vous êtes queen!
wasn't that lion drinking over there?
isn't that a vulture hoisting a snake in the air?
paddlewheeling steamboat to Timbuktu
but first we stop off, in the hot town of Segou
Bambara, Bozo people both give me masks
perhaps my ancestors lived here in the past
sleeping in mud hut Hollywood style
digging the true sound, wow they're wild
balling a chicklet on my second night here
smoking gangha with the chief, drinking later cold beer
morning sunrise tearful goodbyes
up the Niger river aint no millstream
hippos, crocodiles and many reptilian dream
Niger river wide but not always so deep
Malinké children singing me to sleep
endless sahel vistas running from riverbanks
only inhabited by the Peuls, whose goats smell so rank
big surreal trees grow upside down
Baobabs they're called some 40 feet around
Timbucktwo three days, they say
Tell the Tuaregs I'm on my way
Ké-Macina, it's evening wow, thirsty I am

one dollar for beer? I don't give a damn!
that guy there looks like Humphrey Bogart
pointing is a bad omen in Africa, so now the boat won't start
Man, I show am hot and still real thirsty
Lord wont that sun of yours show a little cooler mercy
Moslems saying their prayers, facing eastward they try
ostriches in the distant, magnificently strutting by
yonder is a wild buck and what kinda bugs are they?
Timbuktou, when I get there, gosh I'm gonna stay
Now to close my eyes for a peaceful night of sleep
I count African rhinos not American sheep
Good morning, Mopti, Niger river Venice town
where the Bani river runs into the Niger brown
dog-gone-it, a Dogon! from Bandiagara I bet
down there by the riverside, bathing, all wet
animism and Islam, even Christianity thrown in
that cat's really covered (like life insurance) when death drops in
goodby Mopti, river's getting rough
got a bit of dysentery, life can be tough
taking medical tablets, big ugly pills
daily doses of malaria drugs to drive away the chills
sun bright in the morning, so's my health
when body's O.K., that is true wealth
ten thousand crocodiles waiting for Godot?
all playing it cool? or asleep? you'd never live to know
What a beautiful leopard skin, that Senufo wants to sell
if the fuzz catches him poaching, he'll be put in jail
Ambolore-Youvarou close by Lake Debo
we change from boat to Land Rover, "safari car, you know"
dustheat, dysentery and my eternal insatiable thirst
yet its not Sahara, they tell me it would be worst
so bounce, bruise and bump along we drive
Tombouctou I hope I reach it alive
Look, at that snake crossing the road!
we run it down with our heavy load
water taste terrible, hot and chloride
have to drink sumpin, burning up inside

dry dusty savannah, show aint like my home Indiana
thorny bushes and flattop trees
now and then in the shade . . . 110 degrees
aint no body living way out here
Man, if I wouldn't pay two dollars for a beer
next town reminds me of Horace Silver's Funky band
'cause it has a gassy name, like Niafounke, man!
I lay in this bed, I'll stay in this bed
until someone pours a gallon of cold water on my head
no mosquitoes tonight, thanks to the net
yet it's still hot, sleeping gear's sweaty wet
up in the morning, out by the car
ride hard, on the range all day
I'm a lucky s.o.b. to get this far
Timbukktuu, hallelujah, I'm on my way
road pretty good as far as piste go
twenty foot ant hill, how those things do grow
we cross the river by ferry car almost too heavy to carry
Timbocktoo, just so many hours ahead
Timbucktoo, where the canoe and the camel wed
another Sudanese village, people with a smile
calabashes of goat's milk, ugh it's rank and wild
driving getting difficult and road's really rougher
thick dust in your throats & your behinds getting tougher
as we crush another snake, misfortune drops right in
the Land Rover's axle broke as tho made of tin
pile out into the blazing sun
put on our packs but have to shoulder NO GUNS!
hire few porters for trip to Kabara
we should arrive there sometime tomorrow
single file, S.V.P., and please do watch your step!
"Safari to Timbuctoo," to hear it gives me pep
damn this pack is heavy, why'd I bring all this jive
well everything I brought is essential, helps keep me alive
the elegant porters always sing as they walk
we do nothing but complain & talk, talk, talk
Kabara, at last, just before evening sun goes down

take a bath, eat and drink, then relax in this town
as I lay here in a tent & write as I think
Greenwich Village is a long way off, with its coldwater flat & sink
I have traveled a long long way on the Beat bread I made
now I'm deep in the heart of Africa, the only Afroamerican spade
TOMBOUCTOU . . . . tomorrow, visions in my head
TIMBUKTU . . . . tomorrow, unless I wake up dead
TIMBUCTOO . . . . tomorrow, where no beatniks ever been
TIMBUQTEW . . . . tomorrow, gonna make my own scene
TIMBOEKTOE . . . . tomorrow, thank Allah & all the rest
TIMBUCKTO . . . . tomorrow, overjoyed I must confess

        so now lay me down to sleep
        to count black rhinos, not white sheep
        Timbukto, Timbucktoo, Thymbaktou!
        I do dig you!
        Timbuctu, Tombouctou
        I finally made you
        Timbuctoo
        Yeah! !

OUAGADOUGOU OUAGADOUGOU

OUAGADOUGOU THELONIUS MONK SALUTES YOU
MUSICALLY   FROM AFROAMERICA
WITH HIS   E P I S T R O P H Y
OUAGADOUGOU   OUAGADOUGOU   OUAGADOUGOU
OUAGADOUGOU
WHO SENT SURREALIST ME
TO EXPERIENCE YOU
THE   MOSSI   MANNERS   TO FETCH
ANCIENT BOBO   BIRD   MASK   OF
GREAT GRAND ANCESTORS   THOSE BLACK
DYNASTIES OF THE ANCIENT GLORIOUS PAST
OUAGADOUGOU   OUAGADOUGOU   OUAGADOUGOU
OUAGADOUGOU
THELONIOUS MONK   AND SUN RA SALUTE YOU
BY TAKING OFF THEIR   AFROAMERICAN
LIDS   WHICH UNDER THEIR BARE
HEADS HAVE HID   UH HUH OUAGADOUGOU
THEY BOTH SALUTE YOU   OUAGADOUGOU!

TIDE OF MARCH

Come like the crescent you are
Crescent of sharp blades
Lunar knife cutting a milky way
Marking the night skies
over and above a wide wet ocean
thousands of tremors in colors
crash-water escapes toward shore
Come crescent tide of March
cut beaches from dust till dawn
March on in and over dusty dunes
million miles of tide
controlled or unfurled by the moon

PALM TREE

Tree of great trees
Tree that embodies the spirits of
free giving tree giving tree
Tree who spreads open your upward
thighs offering myriads of dates
dinner dates—night and day dates
dates more plentiful than calendar's
Tree who offers hard on bananas
unskinned back bananas   yellow mellow
bananas curved like the crescent moon
Tree who gives birth to coconuts
and a Joy Juice called legme
Tree that is used for houses, mats,
hats, baskets, chairs, weapons, and shade
Tree who cleanses the breezes
Tree of great trees
   Tree who awaits on islands
        and in deserts where
mankind makes use of your tree
body and tree Juice   without raising
his palm skyward   thanking tree

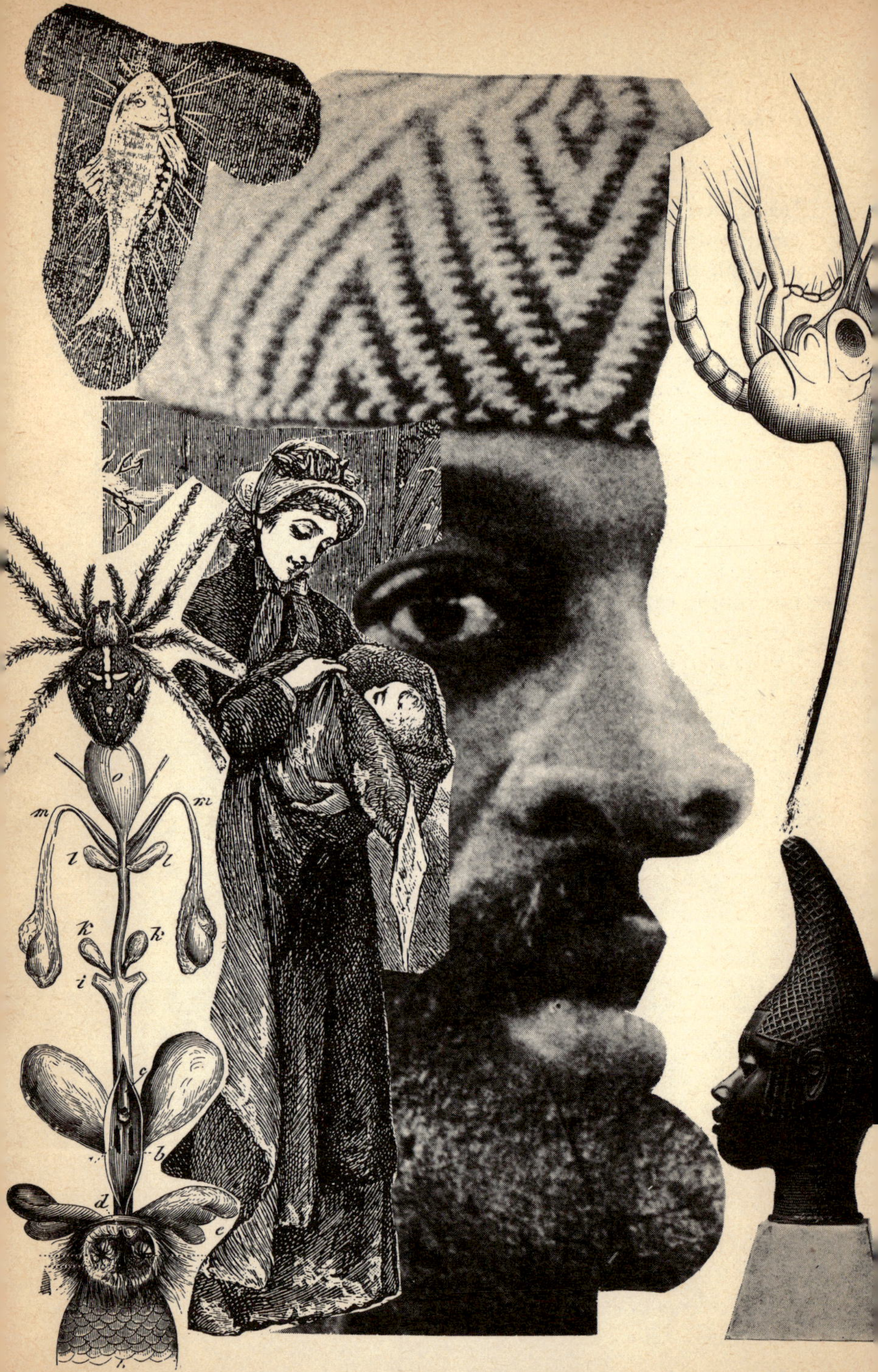
o
m
m
l
l
k
k
i
c
b
d
e

A BLACK FIRST

I crossed the Sahara
hitchiked alone
I crossed
the great desert
made history as
a black first
crossing the Sahara
Someday you'll read
about me
crossing that Sahara
I guess
when I'm long gone
cause so many black firsts
die unknown

YOU'D BETTER WATCH OUT

To Harold Cruse

Our ancestors are watching us
Our ancestors hear every word
Our ancestors know what we're thinking
Our ancestors' spirits can bring us the best
And our ancestors can punish us by just blinking
So we must be seven good things and face East not West
Then our ancestors will allow us to pass their test

GHORFAS

Loaves of hollow bread to live in
Giraffe and flag pole can't come in
Ovals up and under all over
Openings fed by undrunk stairs
Doors of palm tree trunk and tin cans
Ovens cool enough to stay in
Great ghorfas where charcoal smugglers
lead camels by at night.

C_____ C_____   RAIDERS

white communism
white capitalism
have joined forces together this hour
white communists
white capitalists
have declared war on Third World's power
white communisn
white capitalism
both feed like vultures upon Third World's wealth
white communist
white capitalist
both shall receive a violent death

CINQUE MAGGIO

*Dedicated to Ras Tafari
the young lion with bold teeth*

Rimbaud, were you a white man, instead of a poet at Harar? where dark women nursed sick strangers who were a long way from home?

Rimbaud, were you a gun runner instead of an enslaver? in Abyssinia where the sun made your season in hell a bright illumination

Rimbaud, did the ghost of you float to Fascist Rome? Did you witness Il Duce shout his jive from a balcony, always a balcony, especially from that balcony at Piazza Venezia

Rimbaud, you young-fabulous-French-faggot! Did you dig the shit that was being shat? like a long one strain spaghetti laying on the pay-as-you-die Autostrada?

Rimbaud, Emperor Menelik did the trick in 1896 at Aduwa/it was he that founded Addis (New Flower) Ababa/no Russians or Americans had a pink prick in Ethiopia then!

Rimbaud can you hear me? Can you hear me talking to you? Rimbaud!

Rimbaud; Ras Tafari laid his golden medal on Langston Hughes (a black poet who paid a whole lotta dues) The poet later died happier in Harlem than the Lion of Judah shall

Rimbaud, the Fascist, the Futurists, and false Red faces of Italy they broke the Ucciali Treaty! They VENE Ethiopia/VIDI Ethiopia/and VICI Abyssinia/Eritrea and Somalia!

Rimbaud, why did not you write/the frightening nightmares to come? to all of Europe, for it was they who turned a deaf ear to Ras Tafari at League of Nations

Rimbaud, they were there, in Africa, a long way from their home Rome, spreading terror, mass murder, and daily Christian pillage blessed murder on black people   sacred colonialism   church condoned rapine high heavenly military saints diseased brains of General Emilio de Bono and Graziani

Rimbaud can you hear me? can you hear me talking to you? Rimbaud!

Rimbaud, those Mussolini made monsters, they who carried their holy hardon for Holy Mary Mother of White God (old madame non-fuck!) Their Lady of imperialist money and organized religious madness! These pink pig people calling themselves the civilizers of Africa!

Rimbaud, I can not forget what they did! I can not forgive them, nor their children when their children pretend to follow in their bloody footsteps I shall remember the Fifth of May/the Fifth of May/cinque Maggio/cinque Maggio/Rimbaud were you too a ravisher of Ras Tafari's people? Was it you? Or was it the painter Modigliani, the handsome Italian jew? Rimaud? Rimbaud

Can you hear me? Can you hear me talking to you? Should I repeat it again

BANE BLACK

BANE AWOLOWO plain black woman BANE AWOLOWO well schooled woman BANE AWOLOWO good health woman BANE AWOLOWO strong teeth woman BANE AWOLOWO bright smile woman BANE AWOLOWO shiny slim body/naked waiting woman BANE AWOLOWO passionate black woman BANE AWOLOWO BANE AWOLOWO taking my seed I'd saved/loving me full unfraid BANE AWOLOWO I gave you girl twins/because of Africa BANE AWOLOWO IBEJII! You all the greatness of Africa all the forests/all the rivers/all the animals/all tribes/all the art/all the deserts/all the black culture was you BANE AWOLOWO

ZOO YOU TOO!

WHEN I VISIT EUROPE & AMERICA'S ZOOS
I SEE CAGED/FENCED/AND ALL LOCKED UP
AFRICAN & ASIA ANIMALS
I OFTEN DEPART FROM THESE PRISONS WITH
                      B L U E S
I OFTEN DEPART
FROM THESE PRISONS WITH *BLUES*!
WHY DO Third World animals
have to pay . . . such heavy/lifetime dues?

HAPPY FOOL YEAR!!

So New Year/come in!
what have you brought me?
is it strong black music   that one can almost visible see
Is it important black poetry   expressing
what IS/should/and   will be
Is it black magic painting infested with African spirits galore
or is New Year/come again
bringing hard times/bad times   to black folks   once more?

HOME

back
with   my tribe again
i have returned
back home again
glad to be back
with my tribe   BLACK
back   with my tribe
my kin
where mother/brother/
sister/and father
embody all
back where
everybody is
my friend
back with
my black
tribe   again
yes it   is   good
to   be   back
with my   tribe   again

THE BOAT RIDE

You brought over in chains
like a stalk of bananas   ME
in your ship's stuffed hole
the rough passage of ocean
more than three thousand
miles of watery rock 'n' roll
waves slapping your evil
wooden boats with their
white sails and Christian
creed and crosses the whip
the tortures   the inhuman
suffering and losses for me
you did this to ME—America
Britain France Sweden
Holland and those other
mothers I aint
forgotten   Sold ME to
build your colonies to
make you rich and even
today we pick your cotton
or mop your Wall Street
banks   whilst our beautiful
black women display on
TV nightclub their hot
belly rub flashing flanks
But now I leave you
having grown strong and
wise   I go back to my
continent Africa on the
other side   I take a few
crumbs and contacts with
me   also your daughter too
When Africa grows
united, wiser, and strong
I'll tell you what we
are going to do!

WILD WEST SAVAGES

An African village in Harlem
yes but surrounded by electric steel palms with no leaves
concrete and asphalt
steamy manholeswamps
screaming monsters with whirling red eyes
more dangerous than lions elephants leopards
these mechanical hyenas that spit death from their metal gun paws
enforcing their technical order and laws
metal skyscraping jungle
inhabited by colorless wild savages
clad in grotesque clothing
a dangerous group god forgot to give color
they roam around corners and blocks of jungle land
looking for quick kicks
sensational sex
and immediate murder
Riding in and on motor monsters that spew death fumes
these noisy manufactured animals sometimes eat their owners or others
the city savages live high above tar covered swamp
in wall to wall caves filled with mass produced materialistic fetishes
that enslave them
their bodies and soulless hearts belong to these machines and cosmetics
these consumer produced nothingnesses as rewards for 9 to 5 labor
allowing the hung up city savages to lay around on weekends only
even then there is no natural relaxations for them
their kiss is mouthwashed
their embrace is deodorized
the sexual act is controlled by pills and rubbers
after pre-foreplay stimulation, alcohol, drugs, and other gutter junk
In this rotten ruin of jungle/jazz is not heard anymore
only loud bellowing of doom/music eternally electronic
these pale pork skin savages imitate the dark dance under hideous lights
integrated with more horror the doom noise
noise wired into their cold bloodied veins

causing the white pink pallid savage to make death motions
like a rat caught in a high voltage socket
these big city unhip savages
under starless skies of nights
under sleepless days of no sun
their sharp narrow noses run away ——
but carrying them with it toward frozen cold loud hard doom
who awaits these zero beings back to their proper beginning: death
Doom has room for them all
they were too dumb to know
that we were angels
and created heaven on earth   For us all

THE REWARD

HERE   AFRICA   TAKE THIS GIFT   OF ME
I WAS BORN   OUTSIDE OF YOU   BUT YOU
    REMAINED   IN-SIDE OF ME
I WAS GROWN UP   OUTSIDE OF YOU/STUDIED AND
    LEARNED   OUTSIDE OF YOU TOO
I DID NOT KNOW   WHAT MADE ME SO   NATURAL
    BEAUTIFUL   AND STRONG
HERE   AFRICA   TAKE ME   FORGIVE ME   FOR
    BEING   AWAY   SO   LONG

LETS DO SOMETHING

now we know
to bed   we won't go
what is there   to do
between swinging Black me
and puritan Black you
we could talk
we could walk
and make gestures with arms
as we evade/suppress/tell lies
we are false   as we   deny   our
Black natural desires
now   we honestly feel
in bed we should honestly meet
lets get ourselves
together there
instead of
waving coward tongues
in crowded Black   streets

WAY DOWN YONDER

To Nikki and Sonja

When I walked
across the Senegal-Mali
savannah
no Harlem gal tagged
along with me
Perhaps Saphire knew
there was no scene
in Timbuctoo
no juke box loud blare
no salon to fry the hair
no big shiny cars
no mixed drink bars
Just Sudanic houses and
black people galore
Perhaps Sister Soul was
hip to this
and knew the score
thus when I walked
across the Senegal-Mali
savannah
in the hot dust
daily heat and endless sand
I came in love alone
A deserted and lonely man

UP OUT OF THE AFRICAN

Up out of the African
ocean came the animals
with legs as long as giraffes'
necks   and noses as long as
elephants' trunks   and eyes
as bright as birds that
sing   and ears as acute as
scorpions that sting   and feet
as hard as turtles' backs   and
mouths as wide as hippos'
wet and black   these huge
animals of the ocean came

THE PROTECTIVE GRIGRI

the protective grigri
that I wear
that I never take off
is the spiritual grigri
that I hear
that I adhere and believe
As natural as a leopard's
night cough

WE ALL IS

WE SAY HE IS BLACK
WE SAY HE IS COLORED
WE SAY HE IS NOT EITHER
BUT . . . N E G R O
WE SAY SHE IS BLACK
WE SAY SHE IS COLORED
ETC ETC TO CONFUSE WHITES
PLUS UP BLOW OUR TRUE
A F R I C A N E G O

DIRECTIONS

WAKAMBA IN THE EAST
DOGON IN THE WEST
ZULU IN THE SOUTH
TUAREG IN THE NORTH
BATEKE IN THE WEAST
BAUOLE IN THE SWEST
BAMBARA IN THE SNORTH
KIKUYU IN THE OUTH
XHOSA IN THE ORTH
MOSSI IN THE AST
BAGA IN THE EST
ALL AFRICA IS THE BEST
THE BLACK COMPASS HAS
CONFESSED
THE BLACK COMPASS HAS
CONFESSED

THE CLICK CHICK

To my sister Miriam Carmichael, for whom I have undying love, from your humble brother poet

southern Africa   where white oppressors play their trick
on unarmed blacks
shoved from the land   forced in slum shacks
there was a liberating angel
with a trigger sound
a click
When she sings Africa
all blacks become one
making us strong
and even healing some white sick
by just making the trigger sound
a click
Whites cant figure the sound
it's not square but round
(as our black thoughts)
Better done by her mouth brown
real quick
click!
She has a weapon
inside of her eyes
that condemns the enemy
as she sings   this queen
who swings on the enemy
words of a million-pronged ice pick
Her trigger is loaded
when it goes . . .
CLICK!

OKAY, YOU ARE AFRAID OF AFRICA

. . . to those that live by their enslaving sword

Okay, you are afraid of Africa!
you with the long dark overcoat
  " with the wide trouser cuffs
  " with the Moscow autumn wind
  " with the DC cracker grin
  " with the rag waving pride
  " with a cougar's drop of dung
  " with a thimble's innocence near dawn
  " with a plaid tablecloth's obscenities
  " with a lost mustache of wax
  " with a column of Louvre trembling
  " with a flabby belly of British beer
  " with the blood of two kings on your boots
one living   one dead
intensifying the fear you fear
the guilt you grow from year to year

THE AFRICAN OCEAN

Atlantic, they teach and tell us
Atlantic, an ocean they say
Atlantic, even off the hot coasts
         of South America
         and mother Africa
Atlantic, they call it
Atlantic, big blue black wet
        woman of water
I know your real name
    this name I'm proud to reveal
I free you from that slave name Atlantic
AFRICAN OCEAN! AFRICAN OCEAN!
         if you will
A F R I C A N   O C E A N !

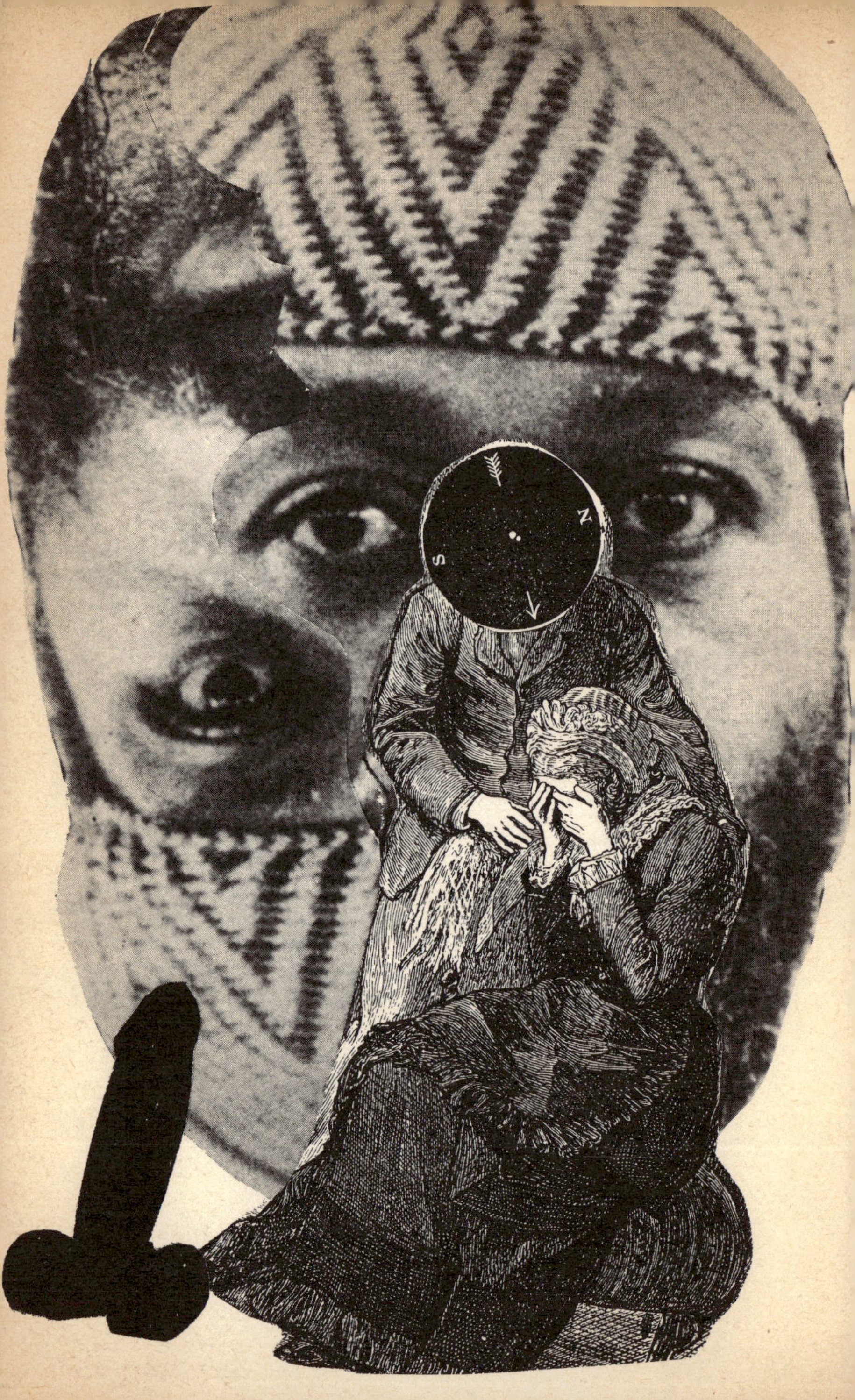
N
S

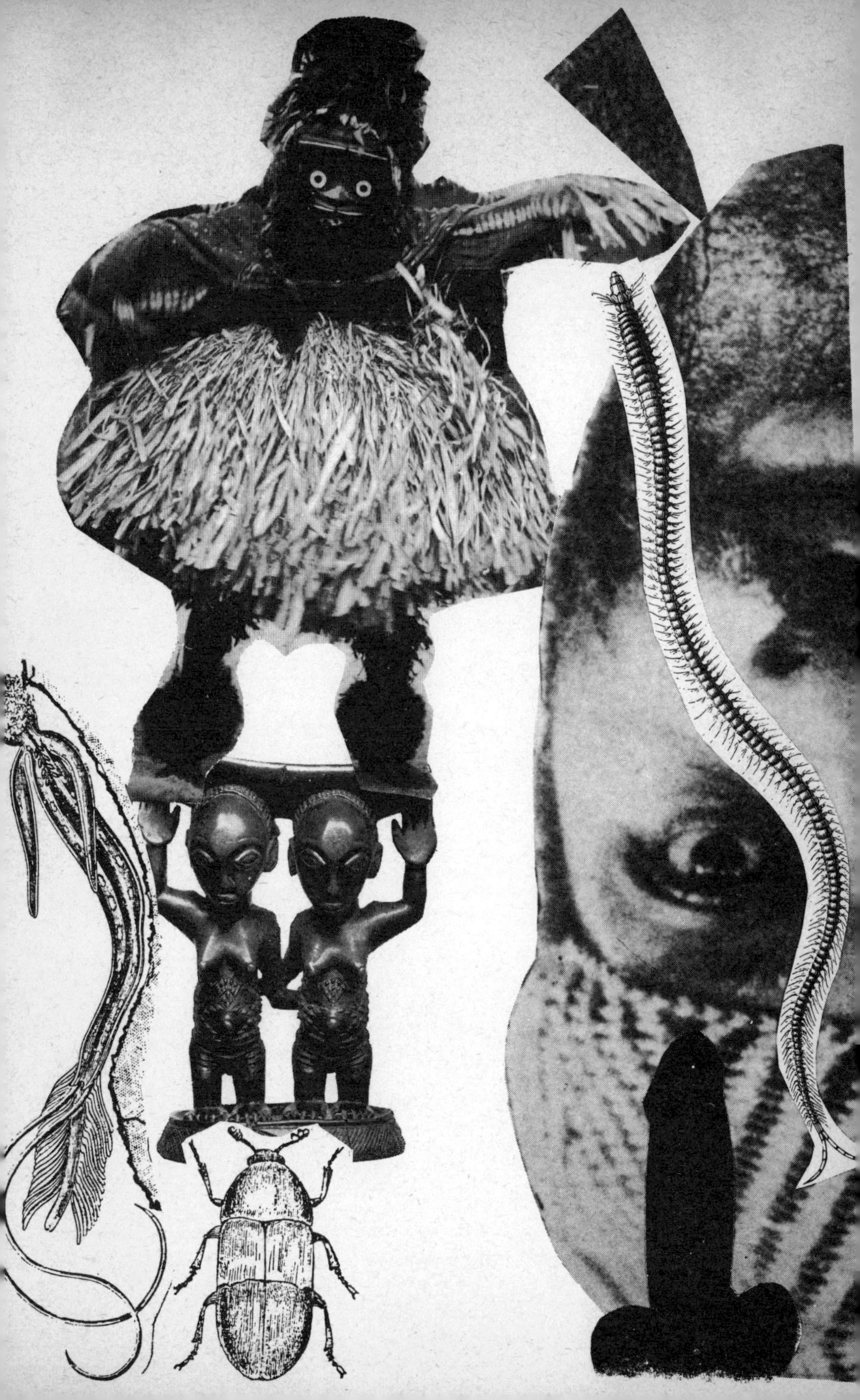

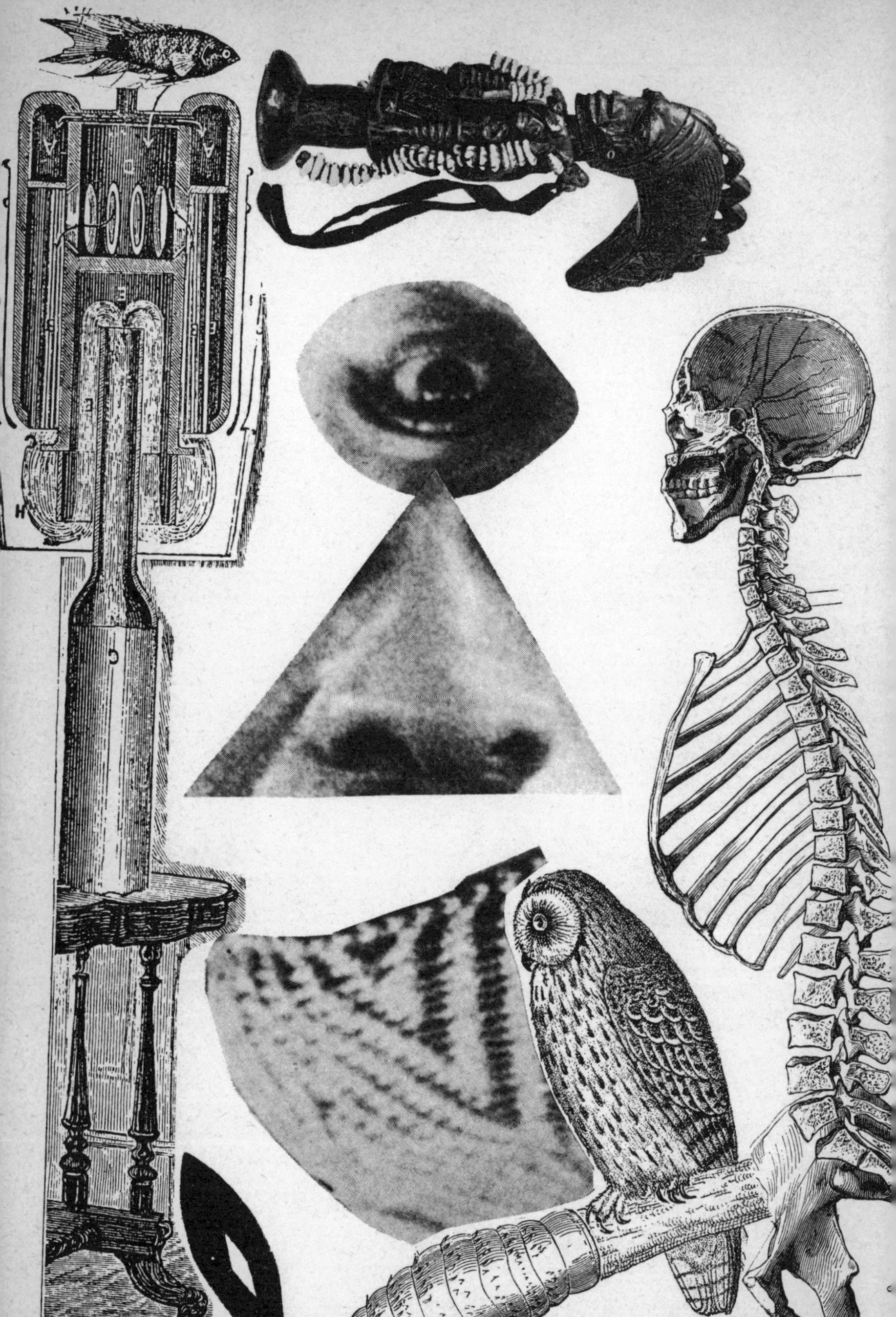

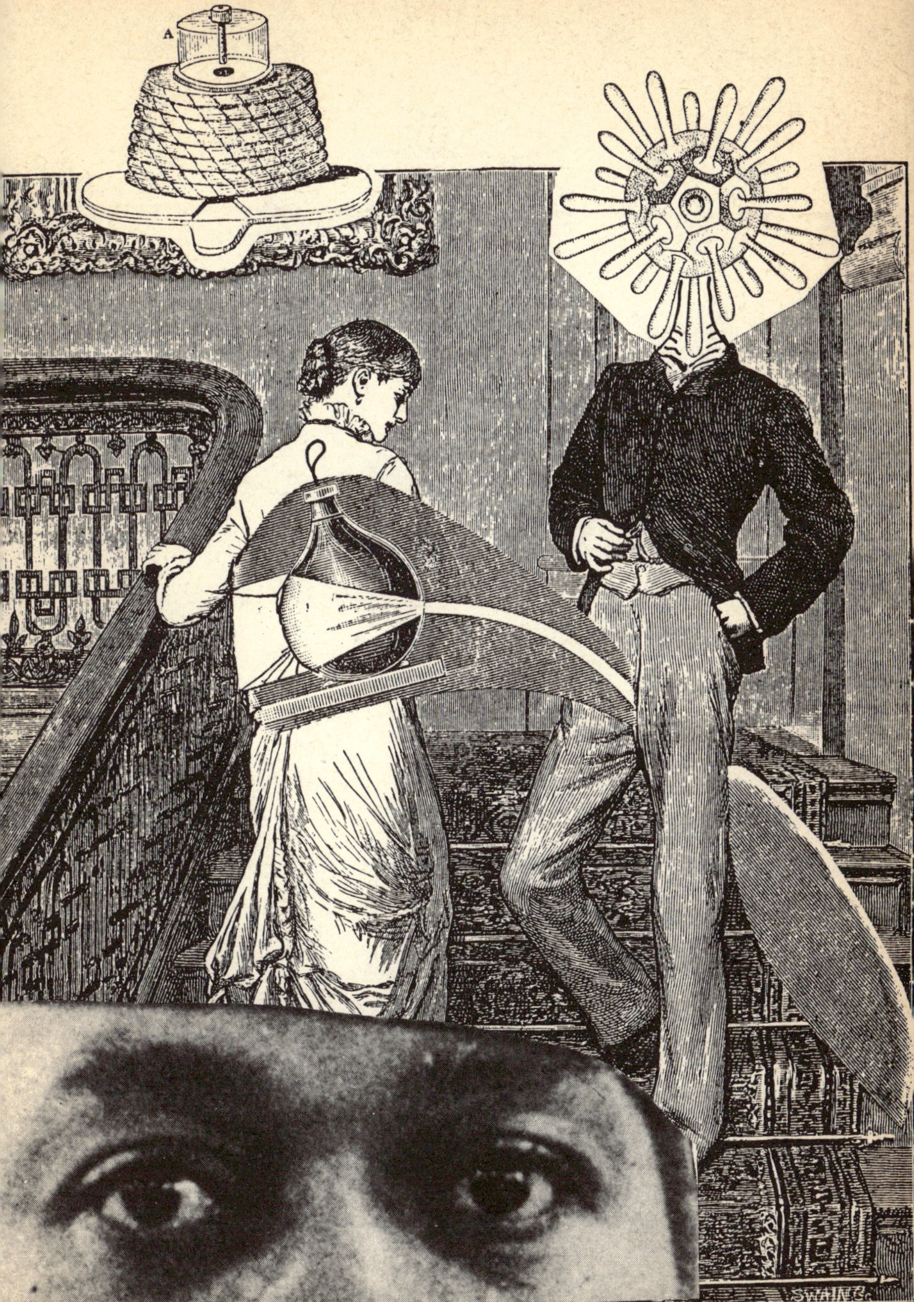
A
SWAIN Sc

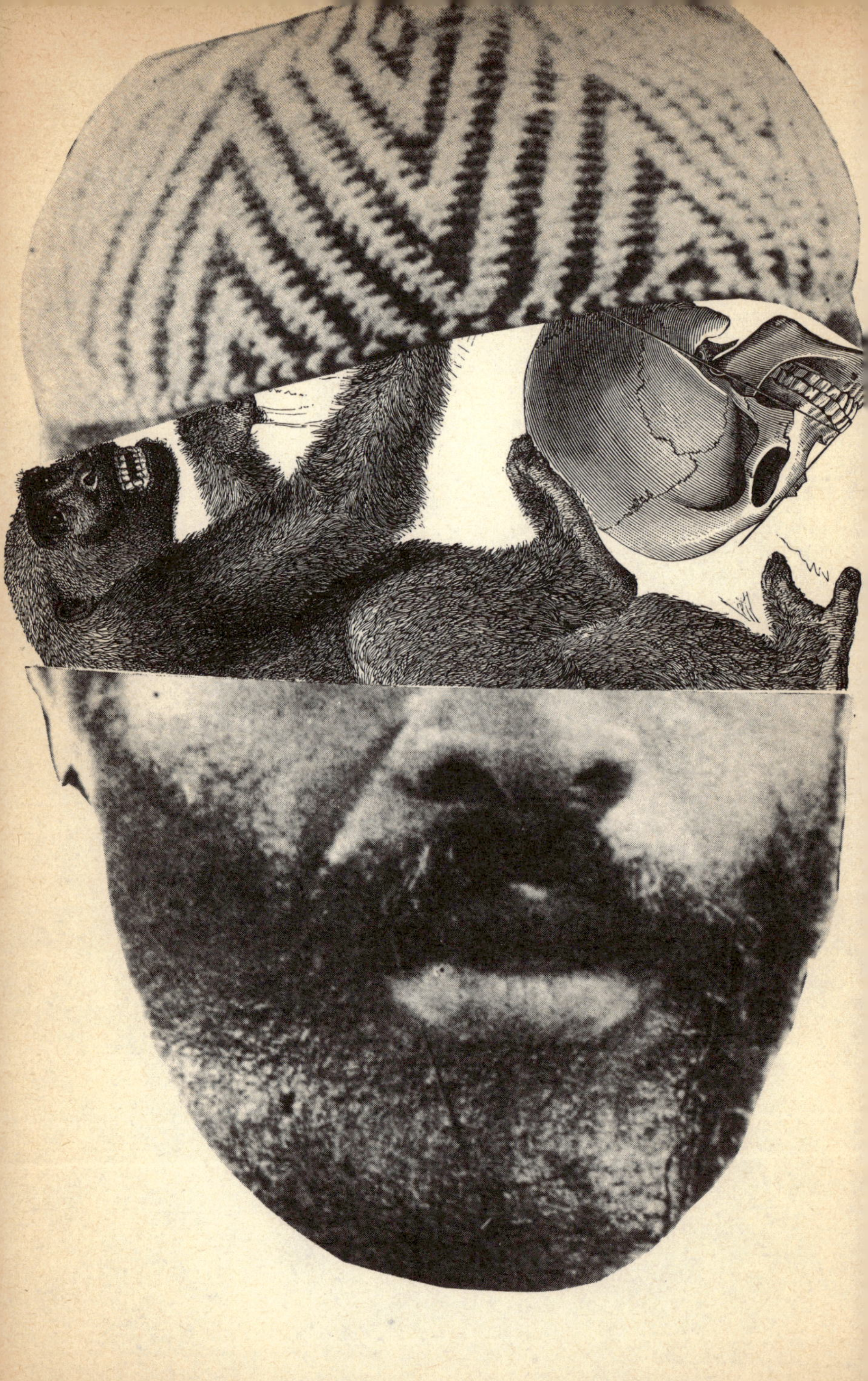

BLACK MANE

he was there this day in Tunisia   old/wise/and worn/
his family shared the space   blessed with two sons
he lays there   proud in Tunisia
antique like a Gericault/or was it Delacroix that painted him
he fought the Romans/Vandals/Turks/Arabs/and indigenous Berbers
he had won   for he was still here   alive/arrogant/and strong/
the Black Mane Lion of North Africa   the last of his cast
on earth   placed in a Tunisia zoo/safely away from you

THE NIGHT OF THE SHARK

Teutonic maid with features so sharp that one could thread needles with them Torn from germany but still dreaming of her ski cap, kraut fork, and Hanseatic weight-lifter
    Legs, long lost from the rest of her body, they sat
    crossed on the edge of embassies and consulates that
    had been closed for celebration of the Sphinx
Leaping frog-car, a Togolese species running on its thought of clearing the Berlin Wall in one great bound, pushing her forward so fast that one had to squint to see her summer smile as she drove by to meet her meat-man
    Torn Teutonic fraulein with hard edge strings and
    fragments that draw lipless Frenchmen in droves to
    her granite single breast under Abidjan sky of bats
legs, brown as grandma's biscuits, they tired of being photographed by ivory cameras held between the teeth of strangers to Africa
    Teutonic-blue-flame-torch-bearer, and sometime angel
    you who subdued the American bison when he'd listen
    with his instant coffee, instant cigarettes, instant
    money, instant romantic happiness
Teutonic child of Berlin ashes and rubble, giving those weak men their tear like an Allied captured swastika flag bleeding from its center as did Herr Hermann Göring's poisoned butt hole
    She lounging aloof in this cafe, that cafe, another
    day another cafe but always pretending Berlin bar
    where crazy customers laugh much louder and real
She a Wagnerian fan in hi-fi, ghostly plans in ghastly Congo dying, saving her beauty for poets and diplomats to discuss, as she sits surrounded in blkivory
    She, a living and dying myth her chosen career, good
    to admire from great distances as telephonic long last
    adventure distances daring not to turn back after that
She, a midnight wanderer in filthy fish markets of the coast, independantly yet sad in her search for one more masculine muscle than her coiled pet python

      She, a fog of the evening with her neon lights shin-
      ing through from Berlin, checking her own Charleys at
      African points enroute air flight with great bats
She, ignoring grey boy of gray death one ounce of sensuality as he staggered through his stingy beer drowning in his weeping crocodile tears an hour late
      She, leading the three (including me) into the sharkden
      we falling her switching Bengal tiger tail just free
      for a short time from Berlin Tiergarten
She introducing the three (which included me) to her brother who lay on his side in a sea of slime not unlike pus and snot from an old tuberculor! She pointing out his measurements that ran far out into the black ivory sea that we saw as we three (including me) ja wohling, uh-huhing, and wowing
      She determined to show us each detail kneeled
      beside her brothers body and opened by force
      his cruel curved mouth thus showing his
      mostprized possession: two rows of sharp teeth
She laughing as vampire-hyena after we shuddered, took the vicemakers son's hand from rose bush, then she kissed her brothers grey eyes that could never close since he had sewn lids and huge gaping wounds received in his battle yesterday with his arch enemy the towering giraffe!
      She staggering from sheer ecstacy from one
      coffin-crate of fish to the next, a family reunion
      singing Tannenbaum tales of Hofbrau hausfrau
She submerged in stench of dead demons of the deep, enhaling their horrible odors mingled with the midnight muscle smells of fishy niggers & boat oils
      She happy as a gold fish in a cats belly, sung to us
      and her reclining brother yet denying the sting ray,
      barracuda and hammerhead whore shark one moment of it
She, reminiscing a greek ship disaster in which she blew the waters into a terrible storm that destroyed the ship and its bouzouki playing crew of rough men who didnt dare touch her for the fear of measles
      She gnashing her dangerous teeth at the huge
      sand dredge whose turtle mother had once blown
      clarinet in her face at a crowded jazz joint

She leaving her huge net stockings, huge net underwear, and manufactured but beautiful necklace which was festered with pieces of scrotums of dead hotel doormen on the pier daring the fishy thieves to steal them

    She returning to her eternally bleeding brother
    instructing us to pull on his great fins, we
    three (including me) obeyed her commands and did
    pull and tug, one would think that her bloody
    brother would curse her but no sound came from
    his coagulated throat She slipped out of her

remaining clothes revealing for the first time her shapely childlike body mounted on her long distant legs biscuit browned color accented by white porcelain ass, she naked now crawled under the shark her brother, and opened her all to him We three (including me) departed slowly across the sea without looking back but recognizing her shouts of amphibious passion

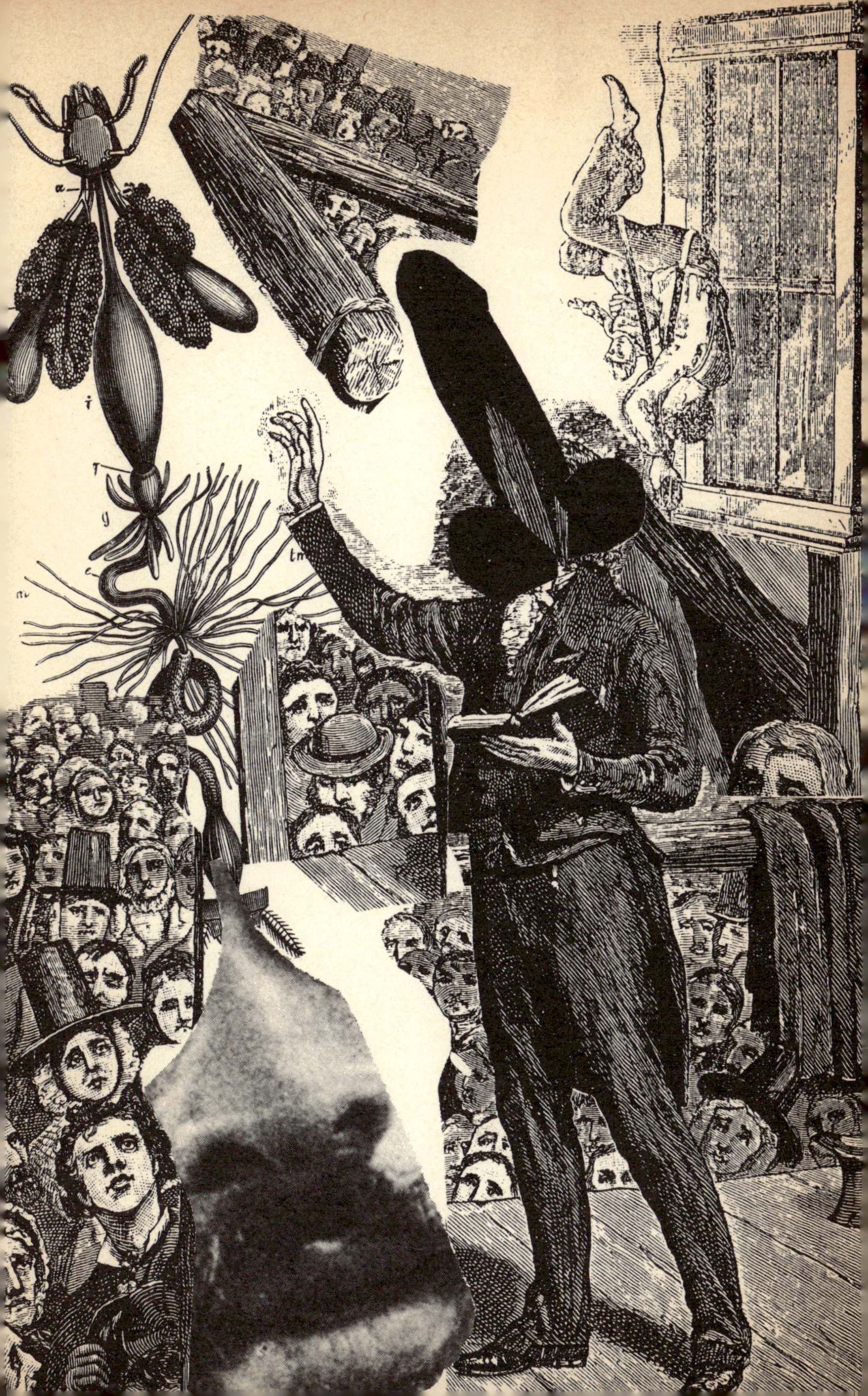

DUTCH TREATMENT

To Laurens and Freda

Holland again
to holler loud again
this time so loud
that they should remember
Holland you little fat flatland
Holland you rich mechanical bitch
I scream
I howl
I pronounce these words
in your golden guilder ears
1619 was the year
do you hear   do you hear
1619 was the year
August was the time
do you hear   do you remember
August 1619 was the date
I scream twenty times
I howl twenty shouts
I denounce that Dutch deed
Holland   Black is
back   in-deed
you sold us like gold
or goats
you kidnapped us from Africa in your boats
I scream   in   Rotterdam
I scream   in   Den Haag
I scream   in   Amsterdam
and in godamn Haarlem
I shout in pain and poverty
for the twenty black men
and women inside of me
Holland hear me   help me

my message travels
the universe with speed
reparation! reparation
for black people
the twenty now more
than twenty million all
in desperate need
Holland you must hear
the price to pay is not
too dear   Pay it now
before its too late   Pay
the price or join South
Africa's future fate!

STILL TRAVELING

> "To wander is to be free: to live permanently in one place is to be a slave."
> —Touareg Proverb

TINABOUTEKA   sell the sick camel and trade skins of gazelles for tobacco

TINTAZARIFT   buy the cloth and surprise the wife trade the sick camel's saddle for dates/figs/and salt return the leaky bucket and get bullets for rifle instead

TINTOUYE   exchange gazelle meat for egg laying hen visit the marabout concerning amulet have birth of second son registered report also the "death" of the sick camel buy new batteries for transistor

TIN ZAOUATEN   return uncle's Quran tell him it was leather bind in Marrakesh but take care that no one overhears this false story but Allah will forgive since its necessary also give him some tobacco swear that it too is from Marrakesh or even Adrar make him feel good tell him that you named your second son after him and that the sick camel is not dead but well stay with him until he is willing to travel then prepare the caravan under his wise instructions on that day sleep with wife to make child take a bath lead the caravan across the sands and rock safely consulting uncle when in doubt write poems along the way on rocks at the finish of Ramadan caravan should reach destination TINBUKTOU (TIMBUCTU) and there we worship in the Sankore mosque   then visit our brother from America   he plays music with us   and gift gives us   and has won our trust   thus we will take him with us to   TINABOUTEKA/TINTAZARIFT/TIN-TOUYE/AND   uncle's TIN ZAOUATEN

BUY AND BUY

*In memory of my
grandmother Moma Love*

A CARGO OF VERY FINE STOUT MEN AND WOMEN IN GOOD CONDITION IN GOOD ORDER AND FIT FOR IMMEDIATE SERVICE
(REMEMBER, do I have to remind you, that only the most powerful physically and mentally, could survive that torturous journey)
These men and women with their children we have given the name Negroes, they have just been imported in the best Swedish, Danish, Dutch, Spanish, Portuguese, French, and British ships. They are not allowed to speak in their native tongue They are not allowed to continue any of their traditions Those attempting to organize themselves will be swiftly dealt with We have carefully mixed all the tribes So communication will be difficult They are of one class and that is slave class Those whom wish to imitate their masters will be duly rewarded Because they will be more valuable on the slave markets Those who seek liberation will be tortured until dead Those whom do not breed fast enough shall be assisted by their owners This cargo of excellent dehumanized animals (I meant to say SLAVES) will arrive by supersonic jets Thus they will not be too exhausted to begin work for those lucky buyers, *immediately!* The two hour flight from America to Africa has proven to be time saving and of course for better health The majority of the women in this shipment of slaves is the United Stater middle age/blonde/blue eyes/and pink pig coloured skin They have been washed of all stench of cosmetics They have been shipped completely nude Thus interested buyers will not be tricked by body paddings/gadgets/corsets/etc Most of them are extremely masculine! But with a little LSD/POT/SCOTCH/GIN/WHISKEY/etc they can be made to breed Those slave buyers whom favor doing the breed work himself will find that it is NOT an enjoyable baby making job one does not attempt to mount the United Stater female slave Those who can afford artificial insemination should apply it to this sexually dull female slave The United Stater! But there are many other kinds of slaves for sale They will be sold Sunday at the

Flea Market in West African Port May the First Prices from Two to Four Hours from 7 UNTIL 11 COME ONE COME ALL TO THIS SLAVE AUCTION BALL DONT MISS THIS GREAT OCCASION WE ARE CALLING THESE POOR PALE CREATURES NEGROES IN MEMORY OF THE BLACKS WHOM WERE KIDNAPPED FROM AFRICA CENTURIES AGO BY ANCESTORS OF THESE VERY PEOPLE THERE WILL BE SEVERAL SOUTH AFRICAN BUSINESSMEN/POLICEMEN/MILITARY MEN/AND HOUSEWIVES TO BE SOLD ONLY TO THOSE POTENTIAL BUYERS WHO MUST SIGN A STATEMENT SWEARING THAT THEY WILL TREAT THEIR SLAVES IN A HUMANLY WAY/THAT IS MAKING THEM COUNT GRAINS OF SAND IN THE SAHARA EVERY SUMMER ALSO IN THIS SHIPMENT IS 1619 DUTCH MEN AND WOMEN THIS NUMBER BEING SIGNIFICANT TO THOSE BUYERS WHOM ARE HIP TO THEIR BLACK HISTORY THE SCANDANAVIAN SLAVES MUST BE KEPT OUT OF THE SUN THEY DAMAGE VERY EASILY THEY SHOULD BE PLACED UNDER THE EARTH FOREVER THERE THEY CAN WORK BETTER AUSTRALIANS AND MALE UNITED STATERS ARE ALMOST EXTINCT THAT IS, THE MEN HAVE ALMOST VANISHED FROM THE EARTH SOME HAVE BEEN REPORTED SEEN ON THE MOON THERE WILL ONLY BE A FEW OF THAT RARE SPECIES IN THIS CARGO HURRY TO THE FLEA MARKET SUNDAY AT THE WEST AFRICA PORT AT 7 UNTIL 11 HOURS ALL SLAVES IN GOOD CONDITION MEDICALLY CHECKED VACCINATED AGAINST EVERYTHING THIS IS THE BEST SHIPMENT OF SLAVES TO ARRIVE IN WEST AFRICAN PORT THIS SEASON COME ONE COME ALL COME YE BLACKMAN/COME YE YELLOW MAN/COME BROWN MAN/RED MAN/AND YOU TOO THOSE FEW REVOLUTIONARY WHITE MEN WHO FOUGHT ALONGSIDE OF THE THIRD WORLD COME AND BUY COME AND BROWSE COME AND SEE THESE SUPERSLAVES THESE NEGRO SLAVES THAT GOD FORGOT TO COLOR AND SOUL SEE THEM MAY THE FIRST SUNDAY AT THE FLEA MARKET AT 7 UNTIL 11 HOURS PRICES FROM TWO TO FOUR COME AND BUY A ROTTEN WICKED ARROGANT WHITE NOTHINGNESS . . . COME AND WASTE YOUR TIME

LE FOU DE BAMBA

Oh chained human being of Bamba
with your turned up truth exposed
for all the world to see that pass
your Bamba sand dunes crashing Nigeriver
Oh fou Oh crazy(?) man of Bamba
hobbling in chains muttering denunciations
while on dusty shelves Mao,
Marx, Lenin and more Reds lay
unread by those   as you uninterested and unfed
Oh chained human being of Bamba
they say you're faster than a gazelle
this Bamba boatstop invades your private purity
thus you wade in the water
shoving slim pirogues aside
walking on water to get your crumbs
braver than six hydrogen bomb pushers
soul cleaner than a child's navel
Oh fou of Bamba
you who fear not
you who have no hangups and no blood on your brow
we are brothers
fou de Bamba fou du Mali
we two know where they are
and we two must break your chains together

THE BLACK COWERIE

Edna africa say:
do as the Bauolé earth
north of Abidjan does
answer my thrust with
cowerie open

Edna africa said:
do as tuareg wells
at Timbuctu did do
answer my thrust
with wetness wide

Edna african edna
never
       discard
our love
dozens of fetishes guard
even now
while
we
are
a . . . PART

BELIEF BRINGS RELIEF

To Bobb Hamilton

the ache
you feel
is an evil spirit
hiding between
your teeth/ear/eyes/
inside your bones
behind your brains
or even under a muscle
this bad spirit
was sent
like a sound or
bad smell scent
so if one pours
libation of wine or
fresh blood or old
human urine to the
East/North/South
but not the West
one rises
with the morning sun
feeling relieved
of the bad spirit pest
the belief can
bring the relief

AS DON TOOK OFF AT DAWN

To Don L. Lee

    Down south along
    North western African coast
    Casablanca the place
    a decadent factoryville
    sorespot of Morocco
    On an August after Alger day
    in a hotel fill
    with hot camels searching
    for humps
    a hotel named Mon Reve

Siberian seals blew trombones
Tuareg headgear and grigris hung
limp above Moorish ladies
and indecent French prick waved
curved blades from Taufrout sliced
bolognee—like Air France arrogance
needles refused to thread themselves
armpits of Marrakesh drip-dry
Oujda throats hoarse with film
photos declared to be just photos
postcards were left naked again
fat ass/face jews of Spain gambled
coins for the blind ran down alleys
desert lizards crowded railways

    II
Sebsi pipes could not kif up
translations a waste of crime
a bag of sand from Ouargala
the rewards of seven devils
trains moved in slow motion

Meknes cruiser from Taza
stiff dick under lunch table
bumped head full of tadjine
overstuffed buses lay kilometers
understaff post offices say no

a fat tear to my lover Mon Reve
she comes swift as a fart
Inchallah tomorrow or the night
a dark staff of life will spear her
she arrives fast as a scent
Inchallah today or this morn
a pair of arms await her torso
she will be here to hear it
she will be here to taste it
she will be here to see it
she will be here to dance it
she will be here to smell it
the smell is stench of passion
stink of paradise on my shirt
beauty of body odor sniffs now
fragrance of fast sweats now
nose blown backwards now

    III
Riff and Cheleuh truck drivers like
tanneries sought hiding places
goat skins! gazelle skins! pig skins!
all screaming skins against police kin
one quarter of head full of Black Panthers
some frocktailed bellbottomed
all disguising faces with sunglasses
molasses lip unhip and shaky
their imported Swedish whores following
thigh gates swung wide for niggers
    Pan African memories Mon Reve

a Casablanca streamline ride
Ibn Battuto too visited Timbuctoo
She be flying in fast like
She be jetsetting to Tanger
She be zooming to Tingus
She be coming around over
the Riff mountains as she comes
Cork trees strip in open fields
palm leaves shake their dates
pine trees cream on their cones
in jubilation as she comes

my love is hurrying its bed
feathers heavier than loading cranes
spread themselves in Arabic
million of fruits become baskets
bats coated in gold dart sideways

causing
her longest hairs to escape her
they entangle themselves in me
my pubic forest is a serpent's lair
one can pull white snakes out near dawn

I sing loud before she approaches
will my trumpet heralds be enough
can moroccans understand her
could if they would at her coming
inspite of translators ridiculousness

Casablanca like Fez on a hothead
Goulimine no longer a cul de sac
Franco's canarys tweet: island!
Portugal will have to die twice
brave warriors unzip their bombs
German tourists sow germs now
Iceland and Australia die quick

brave warriors sneeze their arrows
Polish pig flesh men fry a live
Holland is hollowing for a lung
lungs stuffed with diamonds sink
South Africa dies seven double deaths
Miriam the queen is crowned queen
No more Jo'burg, new Luthuliville
black heroes rise from the graves
sex saxophones serenade the Victory
Archie elephant steps the Joy
      black Africa black at last
      black African back to black
      black power free at last
drums roar from mudhut centers
diplomats' naked chests shine black
protocol: a smile, a touch, a pow-pow
Pan African frying white whales
pole puke rocketed to the moon
white humans despised them too
blonde beings hated their history
blue eye burned down systems
them few who knew what was true
they stained themselves with truth
they turned pure at last Just now
black men and black women too
shoved their canon muzzles for freedom
domesticated two leg and four leg animals
emancipated and desegregated at last
Jungles of the U.S.A. safe from death
blacks, brown, red, yellow, and them
few whites left around free live now
reed sections riff revolutionary
cadenzas causing bruises to evils
children of all colors but one
scatter every where in clean grass
waters of rivers now drinkable
trees are greeted like grandparents

flying creatures police the airways
gloves are free to be frozen now
ice pricks inserted for faggots
guitars hang governments guilty
drums machinegun entire nations
pocket books are not for money
there are no longer bills to be folded
under no account a bank account
not even under Jewish counters
youth and age integrated now
technical inventions used like toilets
sun shines equally all over earth
like the warm smile it is
Ornette and Ellington write anthems
dance movements dusk till dawn

She is coming and she's near
She promised me that she'd be here
She made me pregnant with poem   Yes
She caused me to create her coming
She—my victory—is coming

SAND

Sand in my rice
Sand under my nails
Sand over my typewriter and enlarged herd of
imported rhinoceros (the hairy one from Sumatra speaks Danish)
Sand on books
Sand inside my ears
Sand embedded eternally in sensual candles melted wax
Sand above the bed
Sand sending invitations to more sand to come
Sand swiftly arriving like visible wind
Sand sifting itself of freeloaders
Sand imitating sugar and salt
Sand saying nothing unpleasant
Sand telling me sand stories
Sand warns me   warms me
Sand shifts across my fetishes
Sand writes a page across the sky
Sand roams the desert
Sand swims in the ocean and under a river's pissed in bed
Sand between my toes
Sand outside my Spanish brandy
Sand trickles in by sunbeam
Sand tickles my sweat
Sand in my plate
Sand around my waist
Sand covers my addresses
Sand eats my tracks causing me to be invisible   an unimportant
   nomad with words
I am Just a grain of sand
one fourth of Africa
and spread out
all over this
sandy world

LOUVRE AFRIQUE

To James Baldwin

Dimanche   autumn weather & no rain
Louvre Decorative Musée   no crowd   no strain

one hundred tribes of L'Afrique Noire
yet here one Afroamerican   c'est moi   so far

Dimanche novembre white onlookers admire
Louvre lookers gaze at black art
& some   even feel their fire

one hundred art producing tribes
on walls and in glass cases only one Black
present   amongst all these pale faces

Dimanche grey Paris uncrowded
& sunday Français toujour whisper mute
où est mes frères noirs?
(in their tight collar shirts & looking cute)

Oui, where is my black brothers in their white collars
& Parisian suit   of course I shouldnt spill the beans
& honestly wail   although the truth is
they   are   all
on St. Michel
chasing tail!

I'M ?????

To whites here and over there

I'M THE DANCE YOU TRY TO DO
I'M THE TALK INFLUENCING YOU
I'M THE LAUGH YOU TRY TO SHOUT
I'M REALLY WHAT ITS ALL ABOUT
GUESS WHO?

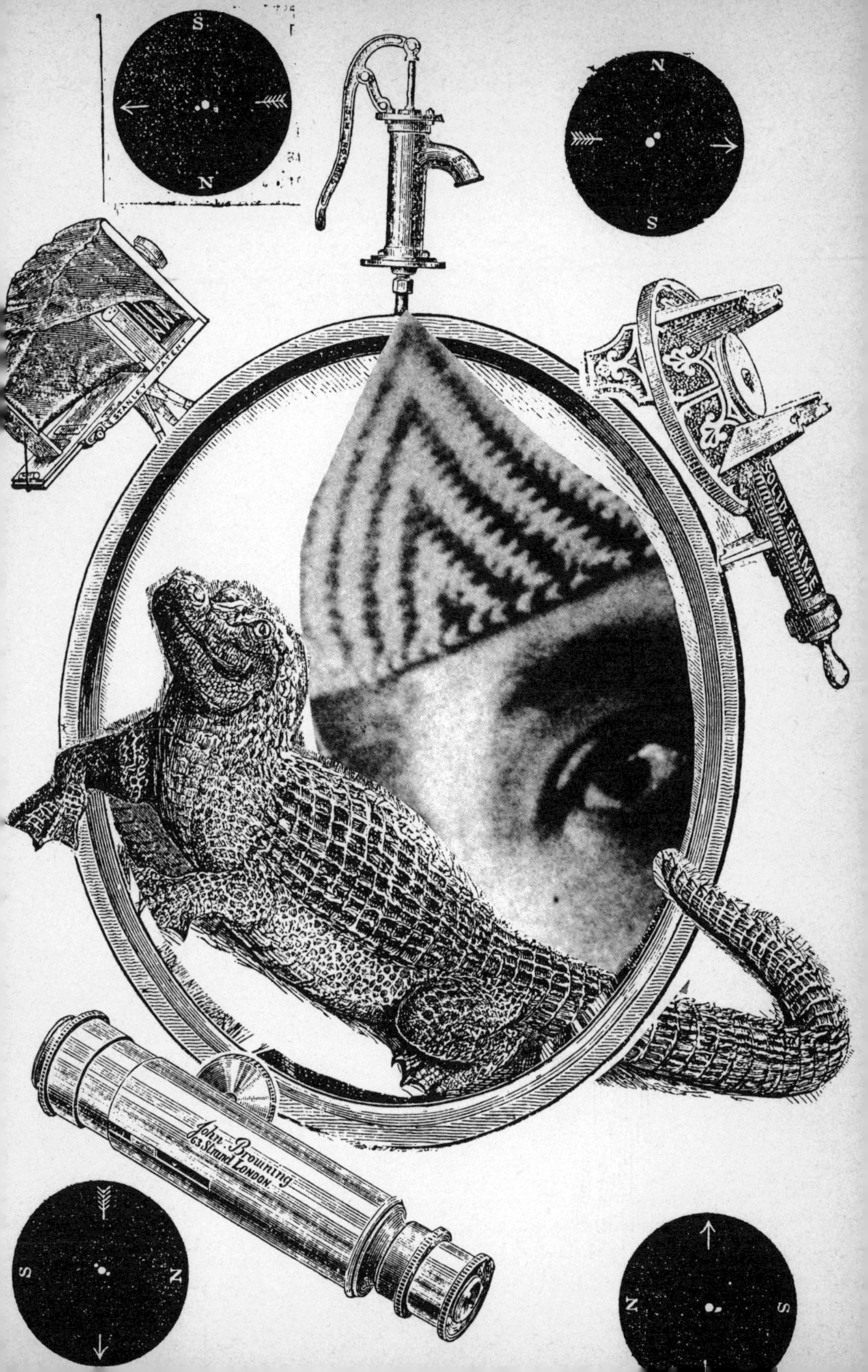
STANLEY PATENT
John Browning
63 Strand LONDON

TANGERINE SCENE

DJELLABA-HEADED hustlers
haunting raggedy headed Hippys
dirty white ankles on Hitchhikers
Volkswagen bus owners buying
fat wallet two hour tourists lying
Tangerine hospitality on display
shops offering camel owners bargains
loud whine of minor key music
full stomach children sometimes beg
no whores to snatch your libido
DJELLABA-HEADED hustlers
wave hello but never goodbye
"Hello man, how are you?
Want to buy . . . very cheap for you?"
questions in a dozen languages
the answers must always be the same
La la la la la la la la la la la la la la la !
Tangier's mint tea and sweet reputation
No no no no no no no no no no no no no no no !
DJELLABA-HEADED hustlers   the Moroccan sensation

HARLEM TO PICASSO

Hey PICASSO   aren't those Moorish eyes you have
could there be a drop of Africa in your Malaguena soul
Hey PICASSO   why'd you drop Greco-Roman &
other academic slop then picked up on my
black ancestors sculptural bebop
Hey PICASSO   dig man how did you know
the black thing would make the modern art world
lively/sing   and actively swing
How Did You Know   Huh   PICASSO PICASSO?

ALL WHITE ON EUROPE
SIXTY-NINE WESTERN FRONT

THERE IS SOMETHING ABOUT EVERYTHING
EVERY WHERE IN EUROPE
OF BEING DEAD
OF FAST DYING
THERE ARE THOSE CHERISHED TRADITIONS
RESPECTED BY EVERYBODY
EUROPEAN
WITHOUT QUESTION
THEY STAND AS TOMBSTONES
FOR EUROPEANS
LIKE AMERICAN WESTERN FILMS
FOR THEY WERE BUILT ON BLOOD
FOR FUTURE IMPERIALISTS TO GLORY AND FLOW ON
I AM SURPRISED NOT TO SEE
A GIANT STATUE
OF HITLER
IN PARIS OSLO OR DACHAU
THIS IS A CEMETERY CONTINENT
WHERE THEY NOW INTEGRATE EVERY/THING/WHERE/
   & BODY
INTO EUROPE'S INEVITABLE
BORING SLOW
DEATH
THERE IS SOMETHING
ABOUT EUROPE
EVERYTHING EUROPEAN
THAT ISNT YOUNG OR
REVOLUTIONARY
THAT ONE CAN CALL
D E A T H

BLACK REPEATER

Dedicated to all my children in what land they may be

REMEMBER THIS REMEMBER THAT AND DONT FORGET
THAT YOURE BLACK!
FORGET THIS FORGET THAT AND ALWAYS REMEMBER
THAT YOURE BLACK

REMEMBER THIS REMEMBER THAT AND DONT FORGET
THAT YOURE BLACK!
FORGET THIS FORGET THAT AND ALWAYS REMEMBER
THAT YOURE BLACK

REMEMBER THIS REMEMBER THAT AND DONT FORGET
THAT YOURE BLACK!
FORGET THIS FORGET THAT AND ALWAYS REMEMBER
THAT YOURE BLACK

REMEMBER THIS REMEMBER THAT AND DONT FORGET
THAT YOURE BLACK!
FORGET THIS FORGET THAT AND ALWAYS REMEMBER
THAT YOURE BLACK

REMEMBER THIS REMEMBER THAT AND DONT FORGET
THAT YOURE BLACK!
FORGET THIS FORGET THAT AND ALWAYS REMEMBER
THAT YOURE BLACK

MY TRIP

I have been to the desert   I have lived with the blue men, the Tuaregs   I have crossed the largest erg and reg in the world with no blues   That was my trip   I have drank mint tea while sitting on my Harlemese haunches after Saharan hospitality lunches   I have hitchiked with my fly wide open and spurted hot sperm into wide pelvic Berber women   I have crossed that vast ocean of earth then created a National Nigger Nuisance hideout in Timbuktu, and written "How-de-do Welcome You" on the Moorish door which is never locked anymore   That was my trip   I have read Lautréamont/Langston Hughes/LeRoi's People of the Blues all the while Coltrane's tenor solo lines drew beautiful black images in the shade of dunes taller than Harlem Hiltons   I have gained entrance into secret societies in Africa: sorcerers/marabouts/and magicians turned me on   They who decorated me with grigris   I still call myself Ted only because you wouldn't understand who I really am now   That is my trip   I have Moroccod/Algeried/Tunised/Libyad/ Egypted / Mauritanied / Malied / Senegaled / Gambied / Guinéed / Sierra Leoned/Liberid/Upper Voltaed/Nigerd/Togod/Ivory Coasted/ and laid her shiny nakedness while my weeny was roasted between full spread Camerouned moon   That was my trip   I found a sacred vagina shaped home in Dahomey filled with foods guarded by two ageless crocodiles and their giant spider wives reinforced at night by billions of white man's grave digger mosquitoes   I have seen a priest shoot the poot out of a rock python near the Dent d'lhomme his skin now hangs in a hut he had a crucifix tatooed across his butt a salute no doubt to pederasty that he practiced   I have eaten watermelon across from Uncle Toms Overseas Cabin when Uncle Thomas came out to enter his big air-conditioned chariot with U.S. Embassy license plate he stared at me as though watermelon he never ate   I have balled a Bauolé broad at midnight in torrential downpour of rain and sweat   We talked to baobab trees that had grown upside up and downside down   I still make whitemen of all nationalities in Africa frown   The whisky faces are tormented in our revenging sun that whispers cooly "burn, baby or run"   That was my trip   I have had goat dung plastered all over my body during a ceremony in the bush Village Voices and Le Monde are used as toilet paper, wall paper, and table paper after being read and reread It is me that has witnessed two hundred foreskins dismembered in December after long stoned circumcisioned dance I too caught in the trance leaping about with no fear or doubt that I am the true savage since I carry the Western contamination That was my Trip I have imitated Pêpe le Moko à la Charles Boyer in Morocco and seen poet Corso cry and tell school teacher lie in the YaCoubi desert I've sung Bambara and Djerma chants to old and young black spirits and saints got high to Hausa wedding tunes and watched long tall basket ball Randy Weston cramped before electric USIS piano I have witnessed thunder, lightning, and wild winds marry the rain a drop at a time Shark girl of Germany loving the black fishermen's after midnight bodies caught in two rows of double teeth Drummers have called my name at dawn African women of ten different tribes wrapped in Lumumba, Nkrumah, Kieta, Senghor and many more cloths I have seen banans prepared for my dinner larger than riding boots of the English Fox chasers That was my trip I have blown St. Louis Blues in Mali and Night in Tunisia in Tunisia on borrowed trumpets Langston Hughes carried my drawing of a rhinoceros to West Africa to enlighten Nigerian love babies with curly hair are called DADA no relation to ole Tristan who the Roumanian Embassy in Athens denied knowing Abidjan has black prostitutes who sell to white fools only as they lay big money in the black groovey good graciousness slits of V.D. in one day or three That was my trip I have been fed peanut butter balls in Dakar dawn by twelve year olds Sacred crocodiles know my shouts and curses Roman ruins have made me laugh to see them ruined in the Sahara sand has been in every bit of food I've consumed this spring this autumn and this long hot restless Timbuctoo winter being offered black thighs for just being back and black from America has spoiled me I smashed a mosquito against my Franz Kline drawing DownBeat covers my toilet seat and a USA flag serves me better as wiping rag I have traveled up rivers longer than white history Boats splash behind hippos like laundromat machines on Saturday St Marks Place mornings Monk, Miles, and black naturalist Abbey Lincoln roar from a loud speaker Those are my discs that are played Tanguy knew me Talmudic jews grave in a distant Marrakesh yard whisper warnings to Peace Corp Creeps In Ouagadougou five days and two nights I awaited you wearing my Bobo bird mask and trumpet Spiked bamboo and barbwire fence around educated fetishers camp prevent feathers from growing under DeGaulle's armpits That was my trip when I hear Albert Ayler in African night along the lonely vast desert edge I scream praises to his sounds I wrote his name on a black stone in Mauritanie André Breton has a statue at the end of Tanezrouft trail Songhai children chase Volkswagen buses giggling black cusses There is rumour in Fado-N-Gourma that I'm just a nomad zoomer That is my trip Timbuctu or Tombouctou is really the place of Buktu a black Bella slave was left at the water hole there Howl by Ginsberg and Rimbaud's Saison en Enfer is not yet known but Bebop has been blown Fat Peul ladies in a cattle truck smiled at wandering me who rode with them for free In old Goa and Agades it took days and days to con a white fool out of a plane ride/money/and four liters of mineral water I have given the shirt off my back, the pants off my behind, and the shoes from my big traveling feet to black brothers to sell for something for us all to eat It is I who walked great distances in zig-zag directions Safaris have asked me to guide them into green pastures I cried for Malcolm X and Bessie Smith in a French barroom I shaved behind my ears in Colomb-Béchar Foreign Legionnaires offered me bread and water for New Orleans memories on horn Ghana trucks with Christian slogans crashed into each other Paul Bowles followed me through the streets of Tangier on New Year night taking notes I onced buried a typewriter in the sand Bamako is much too hot to go in summertime although living at the Grand Hotel is easy Long distant chick from China caressed my hand in Conakry making Baga girls fall in love with me I have painted a Harlem mural on Mali walls for room and board tall chiefs of police listen to my advice about refrigerators and boxes that imprison ice I danced and sang in Niamey Russian workers hate me and tell lies to their friends the American State department cohorts I dreamed that I cut their red necks after a long day of hard planning Blood had dried on blue jeans with a grin Duke Ellington and Coleman Hawkins cry forgiveness from my Japan via 42 Street battery operated phono player English girls volunteer their sex for His Hipness I'm amused to refuse as they abuse and lose Accra is swinging nightly with Hi Highlife dances It is still hot in Tamale like Mexico foodstuff in Ft Wayne Indiana Dig this sweet potato pie I've made in

Kissadougou Jumping down from the big West African plateau Longing to see a television set back into the past Train choo-chooing me through tropical forests German cemetery in Tobruk taking a shit while Benghazi driver looks at American girl's frowns Deep dirty hurts carried across seas into Libya oil fields razor cuts Texas Turning up here and showing up around there after having been several months up Europe yonder confuses the white abuses of the blacks Smiles and deceit can always cheat their fears and conceit Africa big Africa wide Africa is my other side The true side that I do not want to hide That is my trip

EROTICA

"The only cause worth serving is the emancipation of mankind," said the poet André Breton. I feel that Black people in these United States must have a total revolution to liberate themselves, not only from well-known daily oppressions, but self-inflicted oppressions such as acute puritanism bordering on hysteria. Sex and sensuality is a natural fact of most Black people, and only those who are hung-up on borrowed "anti-erotic" attitudes are against the nitty gritty of telling it like it damn show is and showing where it's really at. These following poems were written in Africa and some were created during the Fifties during the (so-called) Beat Generation in Greenwich Village. I was brought up on (so-called) "dirty blues" and spent many a night digging "midnight-rambles" where great Black orchestras and comedians celebrated with creative humor sex and sensuality. Eros is a Greek myth-god's name, but Eros's equivalent exists in all the tribal ceremonies in Africa. These poems like jazz music and jazz dance come erotically into the Black Power bag. If you can dig it, then dig it, and if not . . . ass yo' mammie!

TED JOANS

AFRODISIA

To Aimé Césaire

WHEN THEY FORM THEIR WHITE MOBS TO MURDER
   ME OR SHOOT ME
FROM GREAT D I S T A N C E WITH THEIR GUN
IT'S OUR AFRODISIA THAT THEY HOPE TO KILL
NOT JUST A BLACK ONE
HOW MANY BLACK MEN ARE ACCUSED OF RAPE
WHEN THE WHOLE AMERICAN SCENE KNOWS WHAT
   REALLY TOOK PLACE
IT'S OUR AFRODISIA THATS BEING ACCUSED
NOT JUST A BLACK COLLECTING HIS HORNY DUES
WHERE EVER BLACK PEOPLE MAKE MUSIC DO DANCES
   MOVE BLACK BODIES
OR SING BLACK SANE SOUNDS
IT'S OUR AFRODISIA CAUSING ALL THAT MOVEMENT
A NATURAL MUSICAL JOY ABOUNDS
WHO KNOWS BETTER THAN WE HOW TO WEAR
   JUST PIECES OF CLOTH
WHITE BRAND NEW SHARP OR SECOND-HAND-ME-
   DOWN DUDS GALORE
THUS THE WORLD DIGS OUR NATURAL FASHION
   SHOW
IT'S JUST OUR AFRODISIA THAT
MAKES US IN ANYTHING LOOK DRESSED GOOD SO
WHY DO SO MANY INTERNATIONAL PEOPLE DIG US
OUR COLOR OUR LAUGHTER OUR NATURAL WAYS
   OF DOING
THIS AND THAT ALAS
FINDING US "INTERESTING" OR "SEXY"
EVEN WHEN WE ARE TOO SKINNY OR OVER-FAT
ITS AFRODISIA ABOUT WHAT THEY SECRETLY CHAT
ITS AFRODISIA THAT THEY FEAR/HATE/ADORE/
   (DIG OR DONT DIG)
DISTANTLY OR UPTIGHT CLOSE BY
ITS AFRODISIA THAT NATURAL POWER
THAT IS POSSESSED BY BLACK YOU AND BLACK I

CUNTINENT

To laymates

I want, I shall, I must cross your body cuntinent
I trust that my trip is mutually hip
My tongue shall be my means of travel
Your seven sensual holes will be navigated with skill
My tongue and lips shall chart your cuntinent

I begin by letting my tongue f l o w steadily into your half opened mouth which has issued a visa and carte blanche my tongue gliding into your mouth wanders like a virgin tourist
my tongue sliding around the insides of that vast cave of meat
my tongue caresses your own tongue in friendship
it is your tongue that welcomes the approach of my tongue
in the daylight of your closed mouth they embrace
it is your mouth that is the greatest hangout for my tongue
your mouth moaning its own volcanic blues of pleasure
your mouth flowing joyous juices from all sides
your white teeth some of them blushing yellow coyly smile
your sharpest teeth cannot bare nor harm my tongue's soft touch
our tongues entangled suggest that our lips join
our lips join together in ecstatic rhythms
our joined lips throw themselves fully in this oral orgy
our lips suck our mouths insides
our tongues untangle and watch our lips in awe
my tongue touches your flowerlike tonsils
and finally in sheer madness our tongues say farewell
my tongue glides outside of your mouth waving goodbyes
your teeth gnash to hold back their farewell tears
the goodness of your mouth smells and causes my teeth to chatter my tongue on the edge of soft lips
leaving a soft trail of thin saliva that shines like the sun
leaving your lips tender corners and proceeding toward the cheeks
cheeks round flesh mountains that lead to small hair forest small hair forest

that runs down from the great head of hair forest
this small forest range separates the province of cheeks from ear
dragging my tongue and treading quietly on my lips I approach ear
your ear that saucer shaped well of no sound and yet the greatest authority
    and receiver of all sounds
the ear as timid as a gazelle before a clumsy deer hunter
your dear ear awaiting with all its doors, windows, and portals ajar
your ear wearing a tense grin that causes it to tingle
my tongue deserts my mouth and speeds toward the ear alone
I witness your shoulder come up toward your ticklish ear as it arrives
this tongue of mine that speeds into your ear looking for its drum
magnificent ear of harmless protective fur I salute you!
my tongue enters deep turning twisting and lapping around edges of ear abyss
my tongue maps the contours of your outer and inner ear republic
my lips arrive snorting warm air into your ear crevices
my tongue comes out and makes a pass at your ear lobe
it giggles
your saliva stained under lobe complains of negligence
my tongue like a feather gives your ear unforgettable thrills
my tongue whispers poetry that only an ear can understand
my tongue licks your ear until your entire body cuntinent shakes
romantic shivers cross your face and cheeks grow tight like a fist
my tongue in your ear causes your shoulders to hunch and asshole to tighten
    and of course your perfumed toes to curl up like thin slabs of bacon in
    a frying pan or wood shaving under a plane
my tongue causing you passionate body quakes of pleasure
my tongue causing your fluids to flood under arms, between legs and toes
my teeth nibble your ear but they dare not harm such a prize
exhausted with cannibal comforts and contentment my tongue departs
your ear sobs goodbye from a spent position
tremors can still be felt from the ear orgy that my tongue had laid
your body cuntinent shakes with gratifying gestures
my tongue slides wet from your spent ear
my tongue sets out in the direction of nape of neck
your delicious neck that my tongue will explore
my lips too hunger for that morsel of your body cuntinent
my lips speeded on by rapacious encouragement attacks your neck

*teeth cannot resist sinking themselves deep into your soft neck
like a pretentious vampire they attack a soft neck curve
a bite of love leaves a mark but does not tear or bruise the neck
my mouth sucks like an oriental ocean octopus on your neck sucking fast and
    tenderly swallowing all your sweet pore juices
after what seems to be a lifetime of licking and sucking my lips release
my teeth-lip insignia sensual stamp of approval is revealed
your neck will be lonesome during the siestas without sucking
tongue waves a goodbye by stroking neck with "please forgive us-ism"
tongue lips and mouth set out southward down neck peninsula
trekking slowly south along the nape of warm neck filled with joy
even from this great distance one can perceive the peaks of Tit
Twin Tit peaks rise high above the vast fleshy plains of body cuntinent
my tongues destination is those twin mountains of elastic pleasures
the breast of mammary mountains lips hope to climb speedily
two tits bearing precious unclimbed nipple tops
my lips rave up and across the vast sweet smelling valley of Tit
a bit confused as to which peak of the twin tit to climb
I hestitate
stumbling like a clumsy ostrich trying to fly my mouth rushes up
licking right and left at that base of mount right tit is my tongue
around the base contours goes my lips lavishly sucking
I sniff the fragrant tit funk strengthening my desire to climb upward
your titties grow tense being assaulted by my mouths forces
tongue-lips supported by greedy teeth start up toward tit tip
in the shadow of tit do these carnivorous mouth members ascend
your right and left tit palpitate causing thousands of pimples
pimples from expected pleasures aid the climb up your right breast
my tongue ignores a tremendous tremor of body cuntinent
mouth-lips supported by tongue-teeth lunges upward toward tit peak
the extraordinary tit top the capitol of breast grows harder
it does nothing to conceal its real feeling about my invasion
lips make giant strides toward that perfect peak of pleasure
the tit top welcomes my tongue as the first to mount it
my lips follow and surround the nipple territory
having rushed to titties top thus capturing all of nipple my tongue stabs around
    the base of nipple whilst lips suck tit top*

closing down over tit top with entire mouth forces teeth close in
gentle at first is teeths strategy daring not to scar tit top
rougher tactics are applied as tongue laps back and forth
mouth spreads wide as possible trying to enclose entire tit top
your great breast of beauty that is a target for my mouth
your marvelous mammary mountains making my mouth work
your double breasted full chested pleasure domes
magnificent motions that determine your firm carriage
your breast of sensual comprehensibilities
that first feeder of humanity made to be sucked caressed and licked
from dusk until dawn they welcome my mouths offerings
I suck your tit I lick your tit I caress your tit the both of them
Now leaving the spent and gasping for-a-marvelous-bit-more I depart
bidding a farewell to the best of breast of body cuntinent
I continue south walking on the lips of my mouth
I stop only to investigate some part that I perhaps left untouched
crossing the vast desert of upper stomach I blow and hum
toward the republic of navel passing through the douane of stomach
travelling onward south by southwest from breast I journey on
your wide soft tender and sweetbody cuntinent I kiss at every mile
traveling down the body cuntinent stopping here and there
to investigate thoroughly investigate no precious part should I miss
arriving on the grand voluptuous veldt of skin of lower stomach
lips, tongue cheered on by teeth push rapidly toward the distant woods
these woods are the beginning of that great dark forest pubic forest
upper pubic forest awaiting with all mystery and magic
this magnificent growth of hair leads downward to the tropic vagina basin
down there is where the most sought after prize in all the world lies
down there is why humanity has continued   it is place of birth
down there humidity is a great feeling and smell
down there all is marvelous and each movement is a throw of the dice
dense entangled dark hairs each having been blessed by sorcerers
coiled hairs from earthly hole cover the area
the cave of creation can be found below the great forest
this cave is where truth dwells
in the district of vagina one must be guided
tongue alone can find the entrance into the warm crevice

your body cuntinents masterpiece of treasures this canyon
your entire cuntinent is sometimes jealous of this beautiful soft crack
your cuntinent offers and opens the portal of pleasure for my tongue
my tongue journeys through the entangled forest swift as an arrow
my lips blow warm air along the basin of vagina trail
my teeth sink back deep into my mouth with hairs between them
a giant turtle, a short eskimo, and a broken bidet couldnt be more wanted
my tongue rushes toward the highly sought after prize
your vagina is steaming and hissing a code that only tongue and penis comprehend
your vagina smells of all the great smells that are good for the nose
your vagina tastes of all the great tastes that are good for the mouth
your vagina looks like what a god would look like if there was a god
black magic causes it to move   white science keeps it from pregnancy
my tongue bears no seed but seven thousand messages with each thrust
weak men with turtle necked sweaters cannot tongue their way there
weak minded men with erected tongues and unerected penises are unwanted
it is I who is forever welcome   my lips, tongue and penis
your vagina basin welcomes my approach by opening all for me
your vagina itself winks at my tongue whilst the hairy forest waves
your vagina giggles a group of happy phrases of laughter
my lips and tongue race wrecklessly into the delicious pit licking it with lovely strokes lapping its sides tenderly
your body cuntinent shakes with enthusiastic truth tremors of want of need
your vagina region's magnetic forces pull all of me toward it
your gentle pubic forest of shiny kinky hairs sprays tiny jets of water
your groovy good graciousness lays open like an awesome abyss
I hesitate to describe what this fabulous flesh-hair area offers
I hesitate to report what treasures of the senses dwell within
I hesitate because my teeth, my lips, and tongue are greedy at this point
I hesitate because they would never share this divine part
I hesitate no longer on my journey   I speed onward into the clearing
my tongue plunges into that vivacious vast slit of terrifying truth
my lips stagger downward along the slope of saintly slime
my teeth separate to gather up spare vagina basin bush hairs
my teeth sing a gnashed out chant of joy   hairs held between them
my tongue leads my head down into the warmth between your legs

my tongue is erected like my penis causing your vagina to blush
I have your huge mountain of thighs pressed against my ears
I feel those twin range of inside legs imprisoned my head
your body cuntinent encloses my bodys head
your cuntinent with all its flavors of curves
your cuntinent possessor of fantastic oceans of flesh
your cuntinent that runs north-south as well as east-west
your body cuntinent more beautiful than sunshine
your cuntinent infested with pleasures and treasures
your cuntinent saturated with hair forests and awesome openings
your cuntinent of beautiful adventures during the horizontal hours
your cuntinent of mental love/physical love/and active love
your cuntinent that eros admires and that encourages my safari
your cuntinent that you have allowed my lips tongue and teeth to cross
your cuntinent that welcomed my every desire
your cuntinent is now flying our flag of togetherness from my staff
your cuntinent is under me to bring paradise to euphoria with joy
your cuntinent surrounds my all and takes my mileage and in inches
your body cuntinent that elegant spread of solid space
your body cuntinent my world of travel in search of my findings
your cuntinent that you gave to me
your cuntinent that is now mine
your cuntinent with its every edge and end rounded
your great body cuntinent that is for me to journey on
we have this adventure together today for tomorrow is the climax
body cuntinent I have claimed you
body cuntinent I have conquered your all
body cuntinent you are mine
I place my staff into that gaping hole in the middle of your forest
Body cuntinent! Oh dear cuntinent of contentment/Body cuntinent!!

UNSALVAGEABLE

To J. Halifax

they walk together like strangers
or pall bearers who individually knew the corpse that they now carry
they talk together like prisoners
or like two generals whose vast armies have grown tired of battling
and wish only to go home
they sleep together like grandparents
both dreaming of what used to be
the cavity left by Eros is filled only with tears
they dont touch no more/they dont look into each others eyes/
they try not see beauty any more/they tease and taunt each other/
their days are blank and nights are dreary/the burden of true love
for them is too too much to carry
they desert each other in opposite directions
like droplets from a splashdown of a tear
they refuse to sacrifice anymore
they say   they were weak wrecks   at the beginning

GOD BLAME AMERICA!!

America/Miss America is over paid, over fed, over stuffed and now over here!
America/poets dont fasten their flies no more
America/shoes can not be worn out on fingers
America/Germany is just as strong as America under arms
America/Mickey the Mouse is colored
America/whiskey contains cigarette cancer
America/I lick stamps on the wrong side
America/nine to five aint forever, is it?
America/your fliptop box is showing
America/your women sound like sex starved Donald Ducks
America/the electric chair is too comfortable for your officials
America/I do not want to be integrated into you
America/I continue eating watermelons on TV for a fee
America/Why do I scare thee when I attempt to live free?
America/hot dogs cant be hamburgers much longer
America/Jazz has won the youth of the world
America/rhinoceroses are lonely in the zoos
America/the ghosts of Indians haunt your family nightly
America/many of them aint really ready, are they?
America/Kosher cats closed my contract to you
America/screaming is still valid
America/I do believe you're afraid
America/Munchen maids dance black
America/I sing Round Bout Midnight
America/Your eyes are nervous
America/your handshake's a fake
America/your mask has slipped
America/your whites arent hip
America/their blues aint sad
America/your image is bad
America/surrender to the East! Forget the West! Go it alone, thats best!
America can you hear me? America, did you hear what I said? America??
(a voice) F U C K   Y O U !
America/M A Y   I ?

BED

Bed if you could speak
bed of all nations if you would stop rumbling/squeaking/or
screeching and just say it loud in English/French/Urdu/German etc, etc
Beds of all shapes what you could tell the people of the world
bed whose been slept in/sat in/leapt in/and by the naughty . . .
p i s s e d - i n
Beds of brass/iron/wood/zinc/plastic/aluminium/and straw
we all love in you
Bed if you would spread the erotic words and sounds that lovers
spew while in you
beds of all colors could make most humans blush
Bed you have heard the breaking of wind/the mouth and nose snore/
    and
drifting dreamers gab
Bed you have witnessed the unfaithful wife/the once in a life (time)
the sneaky husband/and the Don Juans fail in you
Beds where promises are made and vows are broken
bed it is you that offers yourself as a playground of pleasure or
nightmare or peaceful sleep
Oh bed   I am tired and lonely   So into you I shall creep

THE SINK

To Julius

the sink is the common white woman
you see her almost everywhere
the sink has two faucet taps some shiny/out-of-order/and grimy
they (like her) run hot and cold
the sink can stop up and make a stink
American white women are drips/some of them pink
one can wash face or feet and some do piss/or pour pee
in the sink
you see her usually with mirror above
the sink with its crooked gut can never reflect true love
tooth/hair/nail brushes . . . cosmetics/medicines/and a glass
the sink is like a common white woman
in your toilet   or in a darkman's past

BIG

Big town Paris. Biggest city in France. Big girl from the states in Paris. Big girl in France at the big time. Big time in Paris is big rebellion. Big girl seeing, hearing, smelling and feeling the big rebellion in Paris. This is a big thing for the big girl. Although she came from the biggest of them all; America. She is having her big ball in Paris. She was always so small in America. She's a big girl now. And she really is a big girl. Big body, big legs, and an old fashion big heart. She is really big in Paris. For in big Paris, the French women are tiny (petite). So she is great big in Paris. Her name is BELLE GRANDE. She is a giant and saint to some. She is a witch and bitch to some others. But she is bigger than those categories when she's amongst the brothers. The brothers are all musicians. Two of them are black. Two of them are white. All four of them play music alright. Belle Grande likes their music because it's big like her. They often create big sounds to give Big Belle pleasure. When this is done she rewards them with a dinner.

During the May-June-July rebellion, which is the biggest happening in Paris, Belle could not buy big vegetables for the big dinners that she often gave. This made Belle's big heart sad. When Belle was sad one of the brothers was glad. He loved to blow her blues on his horn, since he was too big to have the blues himself. But when Belle could prepare a complete dinner, with fruits, cheeses, spices, and big quantities of vegetables, she was happy and loud. This made one of the brothers blow his in anger. For he enjoyed expressing one's opposite feeling through his own music. He was very curious. He often wore wide suspenders and ladies stockings. Big Belle usually watched the big Paris rebellion from the top floor apartment. It was the rented apartment of the youngest musician. He often watched the big rebellion himself. He would stand at the tiny studio window alongside big Belle. She would always put her arm around his waist. He would place his right hand on Belle's big ass. She enjoyed his hand on her ass. He, too, enjoyed having his hand on her ass. They both would watch the big French fight against authority. They would stand at the tiny window until dawn. The dawn was always a big event in Paris. It always took its big time to arrive. Belle and the youngest musician would often lay down in the big brass bed-together.

He would peel her clothes off like a banana. She would please him passionately like an angel. They would create a sensual welcome at dawn. Big climaxes often came quickly. They would fall asleep at once. The other brother, that didn't say much, often came in just after their big climax. He would tip over toward the table. He would not make noise with his big feet. He would be very quiet and careful as he opened the drawer of the big table. He would take out the big plastic sack of Kif. Then he would make himself a big joint. Then he would smoke it. He would soon have a big high. I saw him with the biggest high once. He would take off his clothes and get into the big bed. Belle's big legs were always open. Belle's big body was always beautiful. Belle's big eyes were closed. The youngest musician's eyes were closed, but he was not asleep. So he said when the other brother crawled into bed, "Make it Man, if you can. I'm spent, my dick is bent." The other brother that didn't say much, would make a big nod. Then at once his prick would become big. Bigger than the youngest brother's dick. He would mount big Belle. She would embrace him with her big warm arms. He would breathe big warm wind between Belle's big titties. He would place his big prick into Belle's big cunt. Belle's big eyes were still closed. The youngest brother would sit up and watch. He would often blow his horn or strum his guitar—or even fly out the window. He owned a pair of Techno-Wings. These rocket-Jets attached to his naked back enabled him to Fly. He would never make a big flight, for he was naked. Belle was so erotic. Belle was a big erotic girl. She had always enjoyed sex. She found more satisfying sex in Paris than America. The big national rebellion was a big attraction too. Belle was so happy. She cooked bigger and better dinners. She had sex with the four brothers every day. It was a big thing in her life. The four musicians gave her a brotherly love. It was big and exciting. Belle Grande shared her bigness with the brothers. I saw her with all four of them in bed once. They satisfied, admired, inspired, and supplied Big Belle. She opened her all to the four. They shared their all with Belle. She even used the Techno-Wings and took a Flight. A big Flight-out-o-sight! But big Belle always came back. The big sheets of sounds of their music made her return. Music and bed, dinner and bed, discussion and bed, showers and bed. They all loved Belle. She loved the four and no others. Belle Grande lived happiedly with those brothers.

The big Paris rebellion is no longer going strong. Big Belle is nine months pregnant and the four musical brothers are gone. Big Paris is empty. But Belle's belly is not. A big, big pregnant belly alone. Big lonesome girl. Biggest belly in town. Big Belle from the big U.S.A. Big Belle going back there to stay. Big girl has seen, heard, smelled and felt Europe's all. Big girl has had her rebellious ball. Big Belle's pregnancy from the four brothers who shared! Big Belle Grande. No longer a girl, now that she dared. Belle Grande, a woman, a good one who cared. I saw her once, the night before Christmas—warmer than April in Paris.

KNEE DEEP

to hold my own hand in some secret place away from television
to caress the insides of my own thighs hidden under no clothing
to rub face cheeks against my buttock's cheeks bearing no storebought stains
I standing naked with my nude body pressed against my bareness
I opening my openings to receive my tongue my forefinger wearing nobody's wedding ring but my marriage vows
to suck my earlobe in the shadows of overturned overplayed baby Grand pianos
to kiss my own armpits and elbow my way down into my own spread legs
to blow soft storms of hot air from my own lips down the spine
I lying naked uncovered with nudity wanting everything I can give myself
I opening and closing pushing and shoving giving and taking
breathing hard and shaking rising upward fast tumbling down so slow
coming into my one and only self gasping and gasping hanging on banging on until the cool calm
narcissistic self satisfying ego ridden climax flows gently all over my beautiful body
and I drown
in my own
juices
of
joy

LOVE

To Maureen

love the night   love the day
take off your clothes when you lay
just love just love just love
Love in Africa under a hot tropical sun
love in Greenland on a cold furry one
just love   just love   just love
make love to a friend make love to a pal
love an old white girl
or love a young brown gal
just love just love just love
love in Kenya   love in Kentucky   love in Mississippi & Moscow
if you're lucky   but love just love just love
I know love is not the only thing to do
but love is the first thing that should happen
between me   and   you!

ROUND

To Sofie

ROUND IS YOU   ROUND IS YOURS
ROUND FACE OF WISE OWL BIRD
ROUND SHOULDER OF IGLOO HOUSE*
ROUND KNEES THAT PLEASE MY LIPS CURVE

ROUND IS YOU   ROUND IS YOURS
ROUND BUTTOCKS OF E R O S' DREAM
ROUND WRIST OF CANOE BOAT
ROUND STOMACH WHERE MY TONGUE STROLLS

ROUND IS YOU   ROUND IS YOURS
ROUND CHEEKS OF SWANS YAWN
ROUND PALM OF SPEARMEN'S MATE
ROUND THIGHS LEADING
                  TO WHERE
                          PHYSICAL
                                TRUTH LIES
ROUND IS YOU ROUND IS OURS
              AND ROUND 'BOUT MIDNIGHT
I SUR-ROUND
      YOUR RHYTHMS
        THAT ROLL
                    ROUND
                          MY ROUND
                                HEAD

INTERVIEW

for U

to write an outasight love poem
for your eyes that slant
or your nose that curves
or your lips that kiss
or your hair that curls
or your hands that touch
and your body that smooths my soul
when your voice sisters my thoughts
to write that poem   this night   here   in Paris
with you   outasight   would mean love

WHY CRY

> "Poles apart, like Arctic bears and Antarctic penguins,
> both in the cold, alone and freezing the distances of our pain."

Isolated interests that you do not share
deserted from my warmth
invisible companion
WHY can't you care?
Alone with your favorite things these are
selfish charity some times
caring not about mine
WHY did you go far
Drifting in opposite directions each hour
separation as ink and milk
not feeling anymore of me
WHY exercise such power
Stranded intentionally in body and soul
staying away from touch
silent shadow
WHY is your love so cold

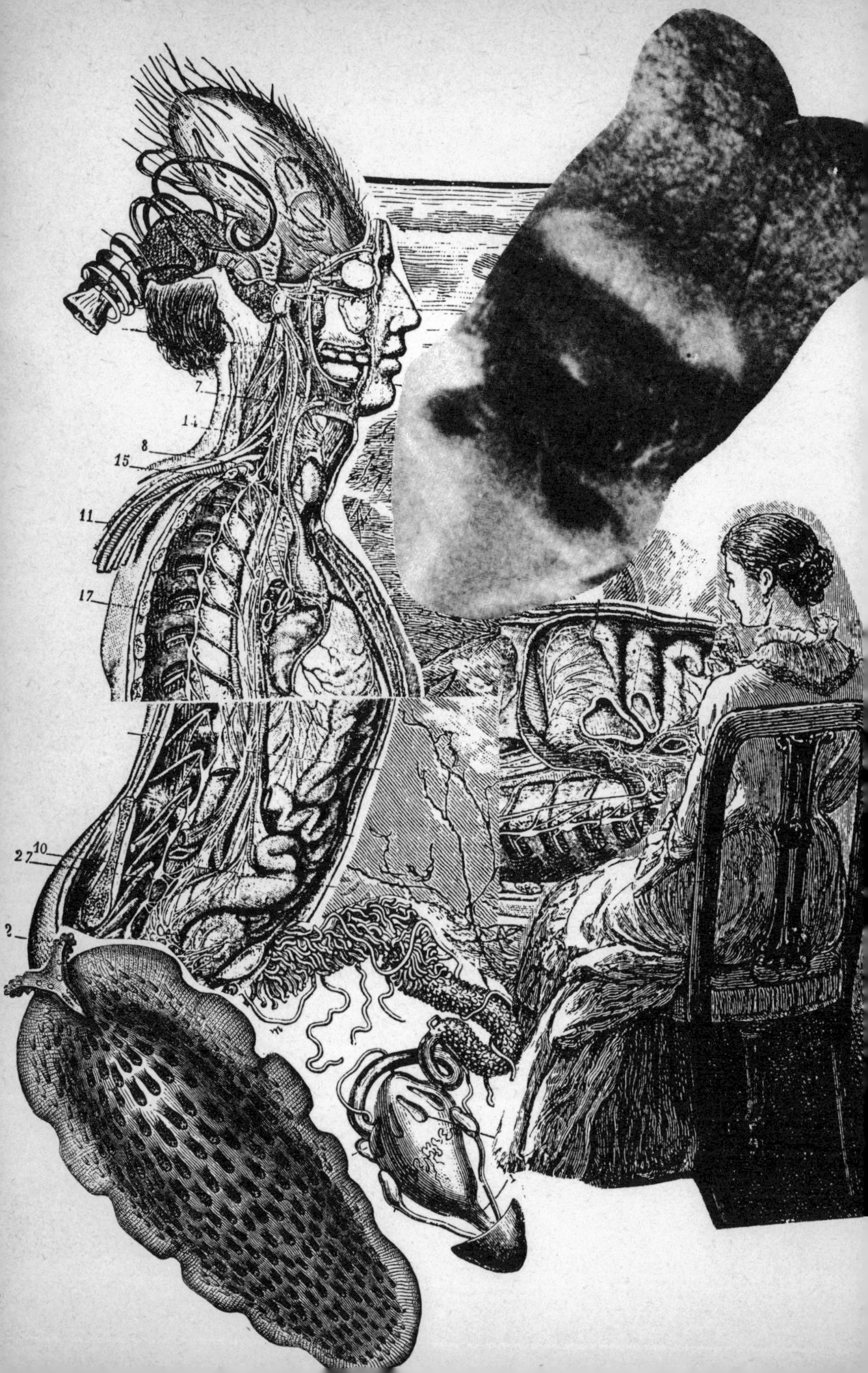
7
8
15
11
17
10
2 7

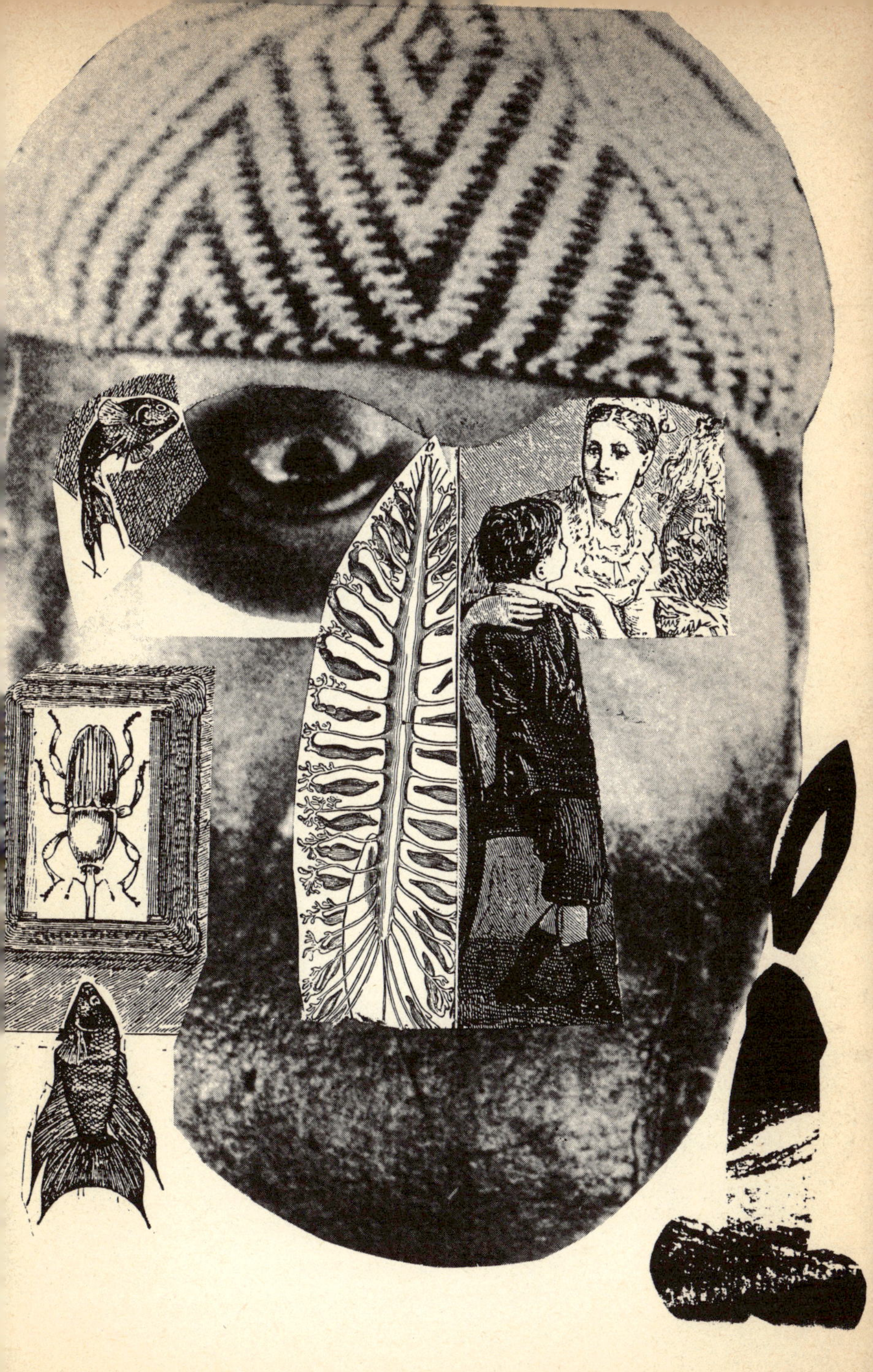

MEATING

To Gwen

You meet
a human being
who could be
a playmate
an every day luncheon date
or better still
If you feel
this being
is for real
he/she could
be
a
lay mate
So
Open
self up
when mutual
moment arrives
let natural
freedom flow
into sex
drive
lay your
he/she
peaceful dove
your "Fuck-In"
may lead
to mutual
world of love.

MY LOVE

My love is like
mountains of the moon
it dont crumble under three crackers

My love is hot
the sun in it shines so bright
that their old Ky. homes
burn baby burn
They've gone with what winds
that blew black flaming tentacles
all through their night

My love is like
moms of the kitchen and titty softness
that is strong in smell and taste

My love is fast
the wind can be seen
if you love me
Its colors never fade like laws
that protect stamps from being reused
with rifles slung across left shoulders

My love is like
nuts in a pile, in a plate, on a table
an assortment of astonishments
in its nutty varieties
sleeves wave as flags
of surrender in New Dixie

My love is
black as the bold soul of my music

My love
enriches revolutionary actions

My love is
and has always been a marvelous surprise for me
It is a creative force within and without
good spirits that I walk, sleep, and talk with

I doubt, like a mouflon near Tiz-n-Tist,
if you could lift my heavy love
It is like a round ball
but weighs as much as seven African libraries in August
Those who love me
try not to lift it

My love can
crush the virgin lioness
who comes with gibberish waterfall mouth

Nashville and San Francisco
with six English towns rest peacefully
now that they are reduced
to white and grey ashes
because of my love
anxious to liberate enslaved acts

My love is like
an emancipation stamp
it can be licked on both sides
sealed on Senegalese Sundays
inside Upper Voltaic envelopes
mailed by postwomen who slip
letters inside their birth slits

This happy fortyone year greeting
rolls up to me on Algeria's coast
"pale men with puke hearts near the moon"
I raise my fist toward the sky
saluting a dove not crumbling crackers
Then I turn upside up
on my downside down love—
This year is sixtynine, my love

LOVE WAY

To Carol White

I love the way
you do this and
that

I adore your skinny
and dig your fat

I'm crazy 'bout you
woman
can't you catch that?

I love you
Just where you're AT

AH-SO!

To Yoko Ono

She showed me assholes, She showed me assholes on eighth of August, She showed me assholes of England, She showed me male and female assholes, She showed me assholes with hair, She showed me assholes of those who didn't care, Anglo-saxon assholes, London ladies assholes, two black British assholes, lean and lanky assholes, diseased assholes, un-at-ease assholes, flabby and tight assholes, lovely and ugly assholes, She showed me assholes, She showed us all—Yet she refused me her asshole—She's Japanese—
                      I am told

PAINTER

To Karel Appel

once upon a time (Il était une fois . . .)
on an easel   perhaps even the floor
an artist   dressed naked   naked mind   pregnant with ideas
pulled out   his long flat & pointed brushes
he twirled them around   in the dream fluid   paint
he swirled this pigment in many sensual ways
the hairs of his brushes
became erect
minutes later   they climaxed
exploded with pleasure
all over the nude canvas
that had been streched out
wide and pure
coming upon the canvas
creations were revealed
a marvelous world
of strength
movement
a great beauty
of its own
now that painting
and painter
relaxes with some surprise
Later the painter hangs in a bar
and the paintings hang
in many museums afar
for eyes

ONE BLUE NOTE

when I was almost
nine months unborn
inside the belly
under the breast
under the maternity dress
inside the vaginal cave
doubled up womb deep
inside my daddy's wife
his steady laymate
    his chick, his love life
    my mother
it was then I first knew
Jazz was a black classical music
that is created each time one blew true

PROMENADE DU VENUS

To Joyce Mansour

I the traveler who crossed Les Halles at summer's end admiring the nude rear of a fur flower from Egypt
I walked with desperate steps looking for the café
       P R O M E N A D E   D U   V E N U S
She a dark slit of beauty having escaped from a large sphinx's paws admired the power of griots in army overcoats from Norway
She had been warned of erected staff of lightning between his legs while he searched for Promenade du Venus
I having been there once during a day dream leaning against a library pushing aside memories of marvelous safaris south
I who had come back black never knew an Ambassadress of Saltpeter
       Where is Promenade du Venus?
She a fur flower agonized by taxi-message-machine-music ignores my meter another Portuguese left his lungs dangling from her eyeball ring
She open and closed her legs to get out from under our thunder urge
       Which way is Promenade du Venus?
I witnessed a naked white curve conceal it self beneath a trouser cuff a crowded vernissage drew like a million ball bearing magnet
I poured champagne across her sand covered tongue until she undressed another Portuguese shaved her armpit in memory of pushcarts
       Is this the Promenade du Venus?
She shoved a cigar between red, white, and blue lips her poem appeared bare admiring her netted legs against the stem of her fur flower
The Portuguese and I stood under her buttocks to avoid her erotic stare
We faking innocence wore children's socks and shoes that hurt
She a female fur flower smiling at black magic of skyscrapers tops
Soft Portuguese Fado sounds emerged from a cellar near Cairo
I the traveler who had crossed Broadway, Jardin du Luxembourg and the Sahara asked the Portuguese as he shoved her under a pyramid
Is this the last step of
       P R O M E N A D E   D U   V E N U S ?

TWENTY-THREE IS NEXT

To Robert Benayoun

Everytime you flush the toilet
   twenty-two litres of drinking water
   goes down the toilet's drain
So place a long dead fish in a dark
   room and it will give off a
   strange bright glow

Each year a comb factory manufactures
   twenty-two billion sets of hair teeth
   thus bowler hats should no longer be
   filled with spaghetti when a bowl is missing

After ballgames are terminated on
   twenty-two hundred aircraft carriers for reasons
   of sexual security perhaps worn sandals
   can be used just as successful as keys to open books

Where men and women have shed their
   clothes and danced to number twenty-two
   on the slut machines in spite of jukebox
   hydrogen warnings—the grass grows
   higher when smoked afterwards

Sausage sack under wears and over rates
   the coming of twenty-three after twenty-two

DEAR MISS AMERICA

To white chicks

DEAR MISS AMERICA
LISTEN TO MY PLEA
HE IS NOW IN VIETNAM
KILLING COLORED FOLKS BECAUSE OF THEE

DEAR MISS AMERICA
I know all about your past
please give him what
he wants   that is
a piece of your sadass

DEAR MISS AMERICA
hear my warning loud
he is fighting mad
and may give the world
his mushroom hydrogen cloud

DEAR MISS AMERICA
I dont mean to funny
but you gotta give up
being square and selfish
give away freely sex and money

DEAR MISS AMERICA
please listen to me now
dig him today/tonight/tomorrow/
and let me tell you how

DEAR MISS AMERICA
you know he's run out of goodluck
so dont just go to bed with him
but get in there . . . dont shuck!

SO, DEAR MISS AMERICA
HERE IS WHAT TO DO
WHEN THE WAR HORN BLOWS
TAKE OFF THOSE CLOTHES
AND LET MR. AMERICA
F U C K Y O U ! ! !

MY BEAUTY WADES

To Grete

my beauty wades
into African water
that kisses Europe's
southernmost shores

my blazing sun
caresses her body
each time she rises
from Africa's waves

my lover swims
off African shore
where sea things sing
praises to her wide thighs

I, a nonswimming poet,
plunge deep into pregnancy
which she fertilized
in this wet warm water

my beauty comes back
dripping with water and glamour
her smile slips into my smile
sand wind marries us
together we dive
deeper into our
ocean of love

JOURNEY

To Katy

some travelers journey
from
East   to   West
other
tourists
North   and   South
yet I
make a   journey
from
your
breast   to   breast
traveling
on
the lips
of my   mouth

SURE REALLY

To André Breton

I HAVE THE SHAPE OF COTTON TYPEWRITERS
I HAD THE SMELL OF TIMBUKTU
BUT LOST IT IN HAMMERFEST
I HAVE EYES IN MY HEAD AND SHOES
MY EYES ARE NOT CLOSED ON SUNDAYS
THEY EVEN STAY OPEN WHEN I KISS!
THE SHOE EYES ARE NOT BLUE YET THEY HAVE THE BLUES
FROM WALKING UP AND DOWN SEEING THE WORLD

I HAVE THE SHADOW OF JET PLANE'S CORNBREAD
I HAD THE LOOK OF YOUR MOTHERS BREAST
BUT SHE WASHED IT AWAY EASTER IN ATHENS
I HAVE EARS IN MY HAT AND GLOVES
MY EARS WILL NEVER LISTEN TO BAD NEWS
THEY EVEN REFUSE TO HEAR TELEVISION
THE EARS IN MY HAT HANG OUT AT DIFFERENT PLACES
ON MY HEAD BUT THEY NEVER SMELL UP THE PLACE LIKE MY NOSE

I HAVE AN ATTITUDE OF A PULLED TOOTH
I HAD THE MOISTURE OF YOUR MOTHERS CUNT
BUT SHE WIPED IT FROM MY TONGUES TIP
I HAVE TEETH IN MY MOUTH THEY BITE ME
WHEN I DO NOT FEED THEM FOAM AT HOME
MY TEETH ARE AT THE TOP AND BOTTOM OF THE WORLD
SHARP AND CLEAN! READY TO RUIN
A RAG DOLL OF DELICIOUS ROSES
I HAVE TOLD YOU WHAT I GOT
NOW LET ME SEE HEAR FEEL SMELL TOUCH AND TASTE WHAT YOU HAVE GOT!!!!

THE SOURCE

To Ricky B.

I WRITE ABOUT
THINGS
I LOVE
THINGS
I HATE
AND ABOUT THINGS
OF WHICH
I ASSOCIATE

THE PASSING COUPLE

To Izzy

the couple past
holding hands
it was
a black chick
and a rich white man

the couple past
talking sweet
dressed all neat
a Chinese girl
and Italian Beat

the couple past
arms around
each loving
other
a tall black hipster
and his wonderful mother

a couple past
walking fast
smiling not
faces filled
with anger hot

like a mechanical
wind up from
Macy's
this couple
that past
fast
were
two all american
racists

ALL IN ONE

To Petronia

I've just
done it to
my woman
my wife
my chick
my gal
my laymate
my lifetime pal
my best friend
again
Now she's
so glad
at me

ADVICE ALPHABETICAMERICA

A is awful unhappy
americans ugly evil
and violent to lovers
that touch lips genitals
or hands in this land
B is over-busy vicious
business that bursts the
brains from competitive
strain bruising manners
of lovers causing them
to balk and rude rough talk
C was is and will be the
cancer that creeps in the
air of america that floats
in and out lovers' lungs in
the food and water filthy
mindtwisting destructive
lowest grade hydrogen dung
D was is and shall always
be death the doom of this
fast built technical tomb
of concrete steel forests
that allows no leaves no
gives but takes lovers'
faith and grinds it down
until its worn out leaving
no true new love to be found
E is eternal evilness
that shines from american
eyes the behind the desk
sharks dressed in money and
zombie secretary spread
evil intentions toward all
lovers that allow themselves
to be near the disrespectors

F is fast life they offer
lovers for money success
destroying lovers' life who
accept deeply their mess
lovers dont live too long
if america's impression
on them is strong
G is gruesome culture
to destroy and laugh at it
all to kill human beings
with a child bang bang
or Supreme Court electric
chair or neck hang the
blood of lovers splashed
across movie screens
billboards big fat books
theatre stages and all
best selling tv rages
H is horror and fear
that lurks in hallways
parkways parking lots
subways nighttimes
daytimes lunchtime
horror haunts lovers
all the time in America
I is the american big
Individual with capital
I causing lovers to die
from narcissism egoism
and my-my- or I-I-I
J is junk of germs
the noise that shatters
lovers' aloness together
the dirty food science
salads to take away the
natural by drugs or jive
promises

K is useless knowledge
that americans learn like
fools on tv and early in
life high schools making
racists of them all in
spite of feelings shocking
lovers belief in each other
to go reeling when white-
black black-white dealing

L is less love is found
in america than anywhere
else on earth thus lovers
must leave or hide them-
selves to survive in america

M is mean murder and
malcontentment in every
american-made corner of
the stolen land the lovers
must be cautious of the
"mean" people the "murder"
people and masses of
malcontent people

N is necessary doings
donts and have-to-do's
these are too tight shoes
for lovers to wear they
are all-american footware
hardware that kills off
love that stays there

O is only for whites
America is where
white men live their
hideous dreams that
cause lovers living
nightmares thus to
stay alive lovers must
in business social life
just jive or stay out
of gunsight

P   is poverty and police
    american's most violent
    offering to lovers who
    put to action the true
    humanpeace and freedom
    reaction to oppression
Q   is nothing queer in
    american but natural
    lovers who are
    looked upon as queer
    for not being like
    america
R   is racism glowing
    like eternal charcoal in
    everything american
    lovers who interrelate
    must suffer the heaviest
    or leave to avoid
    the vicious fate
S   is sex insanity all
    of america trying to
    show off their mental
    ills for true lovers
    this kills old men
    and women of america
    struggling to look young
    their voices whine like
    stalled machines their
    guilty hateful eyes hide
    under dark sunglasses
    making their obsession
    of insanity for sex
T   is torment to all
    from early morn
    sunrise through all
    hours of the night
    lovers are searched
    get leapt on and
    tormented by america

U is U.S.A. meaning
*u*nited in racism
*u*nunited in love
dis*u*nited forever
servicing whites first and
foremost like diaper trucks
seeking new ways and means
to destroy love of lovers
*a*nnouncing that america
is the only way the right
way the inevitable way
to—real—seriously—to decay
V is no victory can
be had by just the
accumulation of money
to make lovers stop
loving each other and start
living for self and money
porer and morer money
poorer and poorer love
grows finally bitter honey
W is waste of life
in and on america
being done by millions
of lovers who float in
the vast ocean of vomit
some drown by sinking its
love into america
X is cross out america
puts on lover that
attempts to live by love
Y is youth who did
not get a chance to
dance with love's
truth but was sent
to murder non whites
over there faraway
every year for white
reasons everyday

Z is for exactly
   america exactly
   american exactly
   all american the
   exact non-love way
   to be to live to
   act america means
   no love for lovers
   america is not a
   symbol of doom
   for love/life it *is* doom
   lovers must
   avoid america

YES INDEED BLUES

I need a woman
to love me madly
to be free with me
and obey me gladly
I need a woman
to love me and be brave
to believe and trust in me
more devoted than a slave
I need a woman
that's crazy about me alone
I need a woman
that's really a part of me
I need this woman
I wonder where she can be
I'll put an ad in the paper
Hope she'll come free

RAINING BLUES

It was raining
The time was late
It was a grey weekday
The clock said nothing
The door awaited to be opened
The bell waited to be rung
The knob was ready to be touched
It was a grey weekday
The time was late
It was raining
and the lover didnt come

WHITE LACE

I met a sustah   the udder day
from a negro college   down south way
this fine bitch   I wont call her name
Said I was too vulgar   and should be shame
Ssheeit . . . I said   right in her face
to this here bitch   of old white lace
we like rapped a luddle more
and den she gits   all mad trying to score
starts low-rating me thinking I'd git sad
but that hincty whore   from a nigger school down south
made me so mad   I almost slapped her in her godamn mouf
but I played it cool, smiled, all evil, and split
Now when I meet another   like that broad I sneer
and murmur
Ssheeit ! !

CHICKITTEN GITTEN !

C'MON GODAMYA C'MON GIMME THAT PUSSY!
LET IT GO FREE LET IT COME RIGHT ON OVER HERE TO ME
LET IT HAVE THIS MILK I GOT AFTERALL ITS FREE!
C'MON GODAMYA! TURN A LOOSE THAT PUSSY, GIRL
LET IT BE ITS SELF DONT KEEP IT FROM ME
TAKE IT OFF THAT LEASH LET THE DAMN THING WALK!
C'MON DAM IT C'MON PLEASE LET ME RUB THAT PUSSY
ITS GOT A MIND OF ITS OWN FURTHERMO IT DIGS ME
C'MON LET GO THAT THERE PUSSY WOMAN!
SET THE PRETTY PUSSY FREE SO THAT IT MAY MEOW
AND JUMP HAPPY ALL OVER PUSSY LOVING ME!!

POSTALOVE BLUES

A LOVER OF LATE YESTERYEAR
SENT LETTERS OF LOVE
UP IN HARLEM
WHERE HE LIVED ON LONELINESS
ON TOP FLOORS
OF SLUMLORDS TENEMENTS
THESE LETTERS OF NEEDED LOVE
CAME THICK AND CLUTTERED HIS
HARLEM HOME WHERE
HE LOVED ALONE
BUT HAD NOT A DIME TO
ANSWER THEM

LOVE TIGHT

PLACE YOUR HAND
INTO MY HAND AND

OPEN YOUR MOUTH
WIDE AS MY MOUTH

AND CLOSE YOUR EYES
AS TIGHT AS YOU CAN

THEN IMAGINE WE
BOTH ARE TWO

LIONS IN LOVE
FOREVER

THE FLIRT

THE FLIRT IS LIKE THE FILTH
THE DIRT THAT ONE GETS
UNDER FINGER NAILS CORNER
OF EYES OR IN THE RECTUM
CRACK
THE FLIRT IS A NERVOUS ANIMAL—
INSECT OF A BEING IT ANNOYS
ONE OR OVER GENEROUS TO OTHERS
THE FLIRT CAN DISRUPT AND HURT
SISTER, BROTHER, PARENTS OR LOVER
THE FLIRT IS THE "MOUTH"
INTRUDING WITH A GRIN
THE "FRIENDLY" TOUCHER
JUST "AN INNOCENT" GESTURE
WITH RAISED HUNGRY CHIN
THE FLIRT IS AT EVERY SOCIAL
GATHERING OR FUNCTION THERE IS
THE FLIRT MAKES OTHER PEOPLES
PRIVATE LIVES THEIR BIZ
THE FLIRT IS A THIEF
THE FLIRT BRINGS GRIEF TO
LOVERS

SWEET POTATO PIE

To Verta

She's got the energy of
the sun in her Jelly belly
her smile lets it shine through
She's got the warmth of
the sun in her heart but
start some wrong shit . . .
that sun can explode!
She's got the twinkle of
African queen in her eyes
the Congo-Benin basin lays
between those huge dark thighs
She's got the tenderness of
mother gazelle's tongue tip or
first drop of rain after the drought
She's got all the healthy
body and selfless soul
like all black folks—and
        should be free
        She's got all she has
        Just like me

JOANSIZEVEN

You are not fat I say
you are voluptuous
as the beautiful days
when Alabama banjo's
strings bean strong
firm thigh high across
Niger river horizon
heated desert sky

You are not heavy I say
you are voluptuous
as velvet in reds, blues,
greens, and pinks
left in cloth tranquility
these things like breasts
taste of fresh coconuts
near cabins of Floridianorwegians
(houses of no gables)
You are not too big
I say You are Just
right size   my prize
you I wear like a glove on my heart

THE HUMP

Mine is long like the Nile
and that river is the longest in the world
When mine is erect it's tall
like Kilimanjaro but no snow cap
I peel it back like a Senegalese
banana bound for markets in Dakar
When it's hard as Ivory Coast ebony
and steamy like a Gabon swamp
and getting drum messages to
go dashing through Africa's
entangle dense forests
I follow its tip that points
toward fat thighs
savannah and there
middle of a bright desert
is an oasis
I fall into this verdant isolated
place (a place of pleasure no doubt)
rushing like a wild beast
mine going in and out making the forest shout
I wondering what the bumpy ride is all about

CHECK UP BLUES

Love, you have lied
and, love, I ask
have you laid
with other "likes" or
past loves?
Love, you have been false
and, love, I ask
are we to be lost?
Are those others
worth our love's cost?
Love, am I
still boss?
Love, sweet one,
it's the time
to make
a choice

MAGIC PANTS

Her panties hang limp and wet
their giraffe, leopard, zebra
and tiger designs relax now
the electric sparks that flash
from them
(when she has them on)
are gone off
they hide their centers themselves
these fancy panties drying there
Her underpants that stay alive
even when discarded for laundry
or left alone on a chair
Her tender yet taunting drawers
I touch with my finger tips
and feel a pleasure flow
that causes my all to glow
Her panties dreaming there

THE UNDERGROUND BITCH

MY DAD CALLS ME ON THE TELEPHONE HE TELLS ME TO MEET HIM AT THE SOUTH FERRY SUBWAY TERMINAL STATION I AND MY DADDY IS FROM THE SOUTH IN OTHER WORDS WE ARE KIND OF BLACK FOLKS THAT WATCH OUR MOUTHS BOTH DURING THE DAY AND AT NIGHT WHEN WE ARE CONFRONTED BY RACISTS WHITES THAT IS MY DAD AND ME WHO ARE FROM THE OLD SOUTH ANYWAY HE TELEPHONED THAT DAY SO I KNOW THAT TODAY IS MY BIRTHDAY AND DAD HAS A GIFT TO GIVE AWAY TO ME HIS ONLY SON A GOOD GIFT LIKE LAST YEAR CAUSE I'M THE ONLY ONE HIS ONLY SON I GO DOWN INTO THIS MANMADE HOLE IN THE GROUND WHERE EVERY CONCEIVABLE BIG CITY VERMIN CAN BE FOUND I BUY A TOKEN GO THROUGH THE TURNSTILE AND BOARD THE SUBWAY ONCE ABOARD I SUFFER TOO WITH THE FEW OTHER PASSENGERS IN THE STUFFY HOT AUGUST LATE EVENING TRAIN BUT I AM VERY LUCKY THERE IS ONLY FOUR OTHER PEOPLE ON BOARD THIS CAR TWO WHITE GUYS WITH THEIR TWO VERY WHITE BLUE HAIRED BLOND HAIRED I MEAN BLOND EYED OH LAWDY HOW I GET WHITE PEOPLE ALL MIXED UP WHEN I AM TRYING TO SAY SOMETHING GOOD ABOUT ANYWAY THE COUPLES WERE NOT ONLY TERRIBLY LOUD WHITE AND ALL AMERICAN IN WILD STYLE THEY WERE WORST OF ALL JUST HAVING AN ALMOST EMPTY SUBWAY CAR BALL THEY WERE: D R U N K THEY WERE BUSY KISSING AND FEELING EACH OTHER UP AND DOWN WHEN I CAME INTO THE SUBWAY CAR ONE OF THE PINK HAIRED, I MEANT TO SAY THE ONE WITH THE PINK SWEATY FACE LOOKED AT ME WITH A FROWN ANYWAY I SAT DOWN AS FAR AWAY FROM THEM DRUNK VERY DRUNK WHITE FOLKS AS I COULD   I DIDNT GO INTO ANOTHER CAR CAUSE I DIDNT REALLY WANT TO NOR DID I FEEL THAT I HAD TO AND THIS CAR WAS

COOLER CAUSE NOBODY BUT ME AND THE DRUNKEN FOUR WERE IN IT THE COUPLES STOP KISSING AND FEELING EACHOTHER UP AND DOWN THEY ALL STARTED WHISPERING IN SINISTER GIGGLY PLOTTING KINDA SOUNDS I DIDNT LOOK THEIR WAY CAUSE I HAD LEARNT NOT TO SINCE I WAS BROUGHT UP IN THE SOUTH YOU KNOW WE IS THE TYPE OF COLORED PEOPLE THAT ALWAYS CLOSES OUR MOUTH CLOSES OUR EYES AND CLOSES OUR EARS LIKE THE WELLKNOWN THREE MONKEYS THAT DONT SEE NOTHING EVIL DONT HEAR NOTHING EVIL DONT SAY NOTHING EVIL DATS US! ANYWAY ONE OF THEM VERY WHITE GIRLS WITH WHISKEY JIGGLING IN HER BELLY AND ALMOST LEAPING OUT OF HER OPEN MOUTH DECIDES TO GET HER WEIRD KICKS AT MY EXPENSE SHE JUMPS UP AND SAYS: WATCH THIS! THIS BIG AMAZON BIGGER THAN ANYTHING THAT I'D EVER SEEN IN ALABAMA OR GEORGIA THIS GIGANTIC COSMETIC PAINTED BEAST OF OVER WEIGHT BREAST AND LIP STICK ALL A MESS STARTED SWINGING FROM STRAP TO STRAP FROM ONE STRAP TO THE OTHER HER HIGH HEEL OPEN TOED SHOES WHICH REVEALED UGLY THICK PAINTED TOE NAILS THROUGH TORN STOCKINGS ANYWAY THIS SWINGING BROAD (LIKE A MONKEY THAT IS) KEPT COMING DOWN THE SPEEDING SUBWAY CAR TOWARD ME GRINNING AND GIGGLING HALFWAY DOWN THE ROCKING AND ROLLING HOT SMELLY STUFFY ONRUSHING SUBWAY CAR THE DIRTY WIND THAT SEEPS IN THROUGH THE NARROW OPEN WINDOWS BLOWS A WHIFF OF HER DRUNKEN BREATH AND CHEAP PERFUME DOWN TOWARD ME IT ALL SMELLED SO BAD THAT I ALMOST VOMITED AND YET IT DID STIR A LITTLE BIT AROUND THE BALLS OF MY DICK BUT NOTHING SOLID NOTHING DEFINITE NOTHING HARD THE SAME FOUL WIND BLEW STRONGER AGAIN AND CAUSED HER FLIMSY CHEAP DRESS TO BLOW UP HIGHER THAN IT ALREADY WAS I STOLE A GLANCE SHE WAS STILL SWINGING TOWARD ME HER EYES THE BLOND ONES I MEAN THE BLUE ONES WERE AS

THOUGH THEY WERE IN A TRANCE AS SHE SWUNG ON AND ON STRAP TO STRAP TOWARD ME HER CHOSEN VICTIM HER HUMAN BEING TO BOTHER HER CHOICE OF TARGET TO "FUCKAROUND WITH" ANYWAY THIS HUGE WOMAN OF THE WHITE RACE IN HER CASE THE "RIGHT RACE" CAME ON DOWN THE LINE LOOKING LIKE A GREEK GODDESS NIKE GONE WRONG OR WITH A MONKEY URGE ON SHE SWUNG HER ARMPITS WERE OF COURSE SHAVEN LIKE ALL WHITE WOMEN ARMPITS AND I WONDER ABOUT THEIR PUBIC PITS TOO/SHAVEN?/HERS WERE CLEANLY SHAVEN BUT FILTHY WITH A MASS OF GREASE: DEORDORANT?? THE POOR DRUNKEN FRIENDS OF HERS SAT LAUGHING LOUD AND LOUDER URGING HER ON TOWARD ME THEY WERE HER CHEER TEAM GOADING THEIR GIANT DRUNKEN FEMALE "GO GIRL GO" THEY WOULD SHOUT IN DRUNKEN UNITY I STOP EVEN GLANCING AT THEM FROM THE CORNER OF MY EYES I SAT MOTIONLESS STILL AND WISHED LIKE HELL THAT I HAD THE NERVE THE COURAGE THE STRENGTH THE WISDOM THE ANY GOD DAMN THING TO J U S T GET THE HELL OUT OF THE CAR!! BUT I COULDNT MOVE YOU SEE I AM FROM THE SOUTH ME AND MY DAD WE WERE BRED AND BORN WAY DOWN THERE WE ARE THE TYPE THAT WHITE PEOPLE CAN PULL A RACIST HYPE AND GET AWAY WITH IT SO I STAYED PUT COULDNT MOVE A LEG THUS COULDNT MOVE MY FOOT I JUST SAT THERE BEADS OF SWEAT POURING DOWN MY BLACK SHINY FOREHEAD FALLING INTO MY CUPPED HANDS IN MY LAP MY PANTS WERE SOAKING WET WITH FEAR SWEAT MY TEETH WERE CLENCHED AND MY MOUTH WAS DRY DRY AS A BURNT OUT ELECTRIC BULB THAT HAD HUNG IN A DESERTED HOUSE FOR SEVENTEEN YEARS DRY AND WET FEAR AND SWEAT THE NOTHINGNESS OF ME HAD TAKEN OVER MY WHOLE AND MY SOUL MY SOUL HAD SOLD OUT IT TOO HAD ITS PRICE I WAS ZERO I CAN SMELL HER PERFUME STRONGER NOW SHE MUST BE CLOSER I CAN HEAR HER BREATHING I SMELL THAT STINKING DRUNK MOUTH I

DONT LOOK UP TO SEE THE SNEER THE SNARL THE TWISTED RED PAINTED THIN LIPS I KNOW WHAT THEY ARE I NEED NOT LOOK HER HUGE MOUNTAIN OF TITTIES FLOP FORWARD AS SHE LEANS DOWN TOWARD ME I SIT THERE FROZEN NOW I AM A LIFELESS CREATURE I TRY TO DIE BUT FAIL SHE MUST BE RIGHT ABOVE ME I CAN SMELL THE CHEAP LIQUOR IT IS ACTUALLY CHEAP BEER AND WINE AT LEAST SHE COULD HAVE GOTTEN DRUNK ON A BETTER CLASS OF ALCOHOLIC TRASH BUT SHE IS A CHEAP FEMALE CREEP AND HER PARTNERS ARE LAUGHING AT HER INHUMANESS TOWARD A HUMAN THEY TOO ARE ANIMALS ANIMALS THATS WHAT THEY ALL ARE THESE WHITE PEOPLE THESE VERY WHITE ALL AMERICAN PEOPLE DRUNK OR UNDRUNK STUNK OR UNSTUNK OR WHAT EVER THEY ARE ANIMALS ANIMALS VICIOUS MECHANICAL ANIMALS ANIMALS WITHOUT SOULS THAT LIVE TO OBTAIN GOALS AND GOLD TONIGHT THIS ROTTEN DRUNK UNDERGROUND BITCH HAS DECIDED THAT I AM HER GOAL NOW SHE IS HANGING ON THE STRAPS ABOVE ME I CAN SMELL HER BREATH I CAN EVEN FEEL HER BREATH SHE IS JUST STANDING OR HANGING ON THE STRAPS IN FRONT OF ME I SAT THERE STILL NOT MOVING A MUSCLE AND THOSE THREE LAUGHING HUMAN HYENAS OF MECHANICAL MANKIND THEY JUST LAUGH AND TAUNT TELLING HER TO DO EVERYTHING SHE PROMISED OR THAT THEY WANTED HER TO DO TO ME POOR ME I AM SO AFRAID THAT I COULD PEE IF SHE'D TOUCH ME I'D HAVE A SPASM A FIT IF SHE GRABS ME I'LL SHIT!! SO I JUST SIT I KNOW SHE IS WONDERING WHAT MOVE I'LL MAKE OR JUST THINKING ABOUT WHAT CHANCES OR OTHER LIBERTIES SHE SHOULD TAKE I JUST SIT COOL A REAL SCARED FOOL I HEAR HER YELL THAT I AM LIKE THE DEAD THEN I HEAR ONE OF THEM SAY SPIT ON THE NIGGERS HEAD THEN I CLOSE MY EYES HOLD MY BREATH TRYING LIKE ALL HELL TO CONTROL MYSELF I COULD IMAGINE HER GETTING THE GOOEY GLOB OF DRUNKEN ROTTEN MOUTH SPIT TOGETHER ON HER SWOLLEN FESTERED

TONGUE BUT I JUST SAT THERE LIKE SOMEONE PARALYZED OR DUMB THEN SHE MOVED HER FACE IN CLOSER TO MINE I COULD FEEL THE HEATED BREATH THE STENCH THE ROTTEN SWEAT THE ANIMAL ODOR NO MORE WOMAN AT ALL THIS THING THAT TAUNTED ME WAS NO MERE WHORE NO MERE PROSTITUTE NO MERE DRUNKEN GAL THIS WAS AN ALL AMERICAN MONSTER PAINTED IN WAR PAINT TANKED UP WITH ALCOHOL AND WHITE VERY WHITE SUPREMACY I BRACED MYSELF FOR THE WORST THEN I THOUGHT ABOUT THE SUBWAY THIS DAMN TRAIN HAS TAKEN SO LONG TO GET TO ANOTHER STATION WHAT TRAIN HAD I TAKEN THIS TRAIN THIS SUBWAY TRAIN WHERE IN THE HELL WAS IT GOING WHERE ARE THE LOCAL STOPS AND WHAT EXPRESS TRAIN WENT THIS FAR WITHOUT STOPPING I SCREAM INSIDE TRAIN PLEASE TRAIN STOP SOME WHERE STOP STOP STOP SOMETHING PLEASE DO JUST THAT STOP BUT SHE IS GOING ON AND ON THIS TRAIN AND THIS MONSTROUS BROAD OF AMERICANA IS STILL BREATHING AND REEKING IN FRONT OF MY CLOSED EYES IT IS TERRIBLE TO FEEL AND SMELL HER BREATH THE HEAT FROM HER ROTTEN BOWELS MIXED WITH CHEAP ALCOHOL THE FRIGHTENING FRAGRANCE OF PUTRID FLESH SHE HAD THE SMELL OF PERFUMED SORE THE STENCH OF PUS FILLED CANCER UDDERS THE RANCID ODOR OF DOOM SHE SOUNDED LIKE A STEAM ENGINE DYING THE GUBBLE BUBBLE OF OCTUPUSSY OR DROWNING ELEPHANT WITH . . . WITH . . . AWFUL AWFUL UNIMAGINABLE HIDEOUS HATEFUL WITCHY BITCHY TWITCHING INSECT INFESTED REPTILIAN RIDDEN . . . WHY DONT THIS TRAIN STOP WHERE IS IT GOING WHAT IS THE DESTINATION OF THIS TRAIN I CANT MOVE I TRY BUT I CANT MOVE I AM DEAD WHAT IS HAPPENING . . . WHERE I AM I GOING . . . SHE SAYS TO ME AS I OPEN AT LAST MY EYES "BOY SAY TO THE WORLD FAREWELL, CAUSE THIS TRAIN YOU ARE ON IS TAKING YOU TO HELL" I SHUDDER I TRY TO CRY I TREMBLE I SHAKE BUT I CAN NOT MOVE THEN AND SHE THIS

THING THIS MONSTROUS MECHANICAL FEMALE OF HU-
MANITY THIS UGH SHE SPEAKS AGAIN "BOY, DID YOU
HEAR ME WELL? YOU ARE GOING STRAIGHT TO HELL
STRAIGHT TO HELL STRAIGHT TO HELL STRAIGHT
TO HELL STRAIGHT TO HELL STRAIGHT TO HELL
STRAIGHT TO HELL STRAIGHT TO HELL ON AND ON SHE
WOULD WAIL SHE WOULD WAIL THAT I WAS GOING
STRAIGHT TO HELL STRAIGHT TO HELL STRAIGHT
TO HELL.

      THE END OF THE LINE
      FOR THE OLD FASHIONED
      THE DEAF DUMB AND BLIND

JAZZ ANATOMY

my head is a trumpet
my heart is a drum
both arms are pianos
both legs are bass viols
my stomach the trombone
my nose the saxophone
both lungs are flutes
both ears are clarinets
my penis is a violin
my chest is a guitar
vibes are my ribs
cymbals are my eyes
my mouth is the score
and my soul is where the music lies

MOUTH

On second sight/the first thoughts of mouth/mouth met on first of moment mouth/of second exciting! of tender smile/the swift sweet expression/of mouth/mouth of first & second/soulful invitings! mouth of gestures/mouth of questions/mouth of want/mouth of silence/ mouth of truth/mouth of smiles/mouth of lies/mouth of need/mouth of tranquils/mouth of greetings/mouth of answers/mouth of song/ mouth of cries/mouth of moans/mouth of chatter/mouth of mystery/ A MOUTH OF M A T T E R!!

COOL

I find myself in bed. I am not at home again. I open one eye and I see the chick that I had made it with. I open the other eye and I see that it is half past eleven. I open my mouth and yawn. I taste her in my saliva. I look at her to remember. I remember now. I also remember her name. I often forget names. I wake up frequently in strange beds. I have never been surprised. I seldom sleep at home anymore. I glance at the wall. I see a painting. It is the rhinoceros painting that I gave her. I look across and around her pad. I like it very much. I see her neighbors through the window. They are outside in the garden. I dont dig her neighbors. I know they dont dig me. I want to dig everybody and yet . . . her neighbors is somethin' else! I look at my chick again. She is snoring away. She has a tan on her round pink face. She has a sensual smile on her lips. I think women are twice as beautiful while they sleep. I lean over and kiss those lips. I kiss her softly. I dig kissing! I put my arm around her sleeping body. She is my own private sleeping beauty. I kiss her again. She stirs a bit. I hold her tighter. Her body smells excite me. I embrace her passionately. I dig embracing! She is awakened and pushes her self closer to me. We embrace. Our bodies are united as one. I kiss her with my mouth open. She parts her lips. I taste me inside her mouth. She opens one eye. She swoons and clings to me. I can see her eyes sparkling. I ease my tongue into her mouth. She tastes of last nights pleasures. I feel her teeth threatening my tongue. I withdraw my tongue. We stop kissing. We lay there looking at each other. I smile at her. She smiles and says good morning. I laugh and say good afternoon. We both laugh. I dig laughter! She kisses me hard on the lips. I hold her tighter. She reaches for the phonograph. It begins to play. I say . . . wow baby how cool. She smiles and says Miles Davis in the morning! Miles Davis is blowing a funky early morning blues. I look at her. She is very happy. I am happy. We are both happy together. I dig being happy! We both dig the jazz of Miles Davis. We lay back and listen. We look at each other as we listen. I dig her and she digs me. We have had a great night together. The music is augmenting our pleasures. I watch her blonde head move rhythmicly with the music. We are both entraced by it. Jazz music is a magic spell binder. We are both swinging.

Her rude neighbors turn on their radio. They are still outside the window in the garden. They deliberately set their loud radio near our window. It is so loud that we have to turn our phonograph off. Their radio is blaring ridiculous commercial and stale musics. And we had been digging jazz which is a fresh American music. Their radio seems to get louder. We both shrugged our naked shoulders. We start kissing and feeling again. We are both excited. Her rude neighbors turn down their radio. I hear the man say, "I can not figure, since she's such a nice girl . . . why a nigger!" My chick looks at me and smiles. I kiss her on those marvelous lips. I still dig her. We embrace some more and then some more. We dig embracing. The neighbors turn up their radio again. The stale commercial music is blaring. But it is suddenly interrupted. A voice on the radio speaks rapidly and excitedly. The voice says: WAR HAS BEEN DECLARED!! EVERY AMERICAN CITIZEN MUST TAKE COVER/RUN IMMEDIATELY TO YOUR FALLOUT SHELTER TAKE YOUR SURVIVAL KIT WITH YOU/ FAMILY UNITS SHOULD DEFECATE AND URINATE NOW BEFORE THEY EVACUATE/THOSE IN THE SOUTH MUST NOT SEGREGATE DURING THIS GRAVE EMERGENCY/THE PRESIDENT WISHES EVERY AMERICAN THE BEST OF LUCK/ ENEMY MISSILES ARE APPROACHING FASTER THAN OUR ANTI MISSILE MISSILES CAN TRACK THEM!!!!! I hear her neighbors scream. A cold chill runs through me. My chicks cuddles in my arms. I tell her, "We're together baby and in love." I see her neighbors scramble in the garden. The man slips and falls to his knees. So finding himself in this position he begins to pray. I overhear him. He prays loud and scary. He yells; Lord! God! Jehovah! Christ! Allah! Heavenly Father, forgive me, forgive us, dear God you've made a great mistake. WE ARE GOD LOVING AMERICANS. WE ARE WHITE AND CHRISTIANS! WE BELONG TO THE CHURCH! WE'VE DONE SEEN THE LIGHT! OH GOD YOU'VE GOOFED/PLEASE DEAR GOD GOD DONT LET THIS HAPPEN TO US/WE ARE AMERICANS!!!!!!! They all scramble down into the basement. I can hear them falling over pingpong tables and other leisure crap. I hear the women crying and pleading. They are in the basement but still trying to hide. There is no place to hide. Death can find anybody, anytime and anyplace. There is no escape from death. The scene is very sad. My chick looks at me. I look at her. I can see she is not frightened. I smile. She smiles. We are both smiling. I dig smiling! She reaches toward the phonograph. It begins to play. Miles Davis is blowing again. She kisses me. I hold her tight. The jazz is very soothing. I love jazz. She loves jazz. Jazz is our religion! So we lie there. In the darkness of her pad. Digging jazz. And in love. And waiting for the H-Bomb. And so we lied there, and died there, together . . . but extra cool.

125 WAYS TO SEX OR SEXPLOSION

prudish sex   impotent sex   pretty sex   important sex   paper sex   good sex   peace sex   war sex   play sex   poor sex   rich sex   race sex   win sex   free sex   slave sex   blonde sex   bald sex   big sex   little sex   clean sex   dirty sex   funky sex   fair sex   ofay sex   maumau sex   club sex   hotel sex   motel sex   his sex   her sex   Yankee sex   captain sex   sergeant sex   private sex   spade sex   cool sex   safe sex   slavic sex   new sex   old sex   antique sex   blue sex   in sex   young sex   soft sex   hard sex   hate sex   sin sex   middle sex   bottom sex   chick sex   bitch sex   blind sex   out sex   naked sex   nice sex   neat sex   cryptic sex   civil sex   green sex   cruel sex   spring sex   summer sex   back seat car sex   sandy beach sex   ice cream soda sex   convertible car sex   hospital ward sex   pay-as-you-go sex   one dollar down sex   no credit today sex   below cost sex   supermarket sex   movie balcony sex   bad news sex   cover girl sex   colored man sex   Paris sex   Amsterdam sex   Berlin sex   Copenhagen sex   Oslo sex   Athens sex   Vienna sex   day-in-Daker sex   night-in-Tunisia sex   'round bout midnite sex   straight no chasing sex   Timbuctu sex   Tangier sex   Ougadougou sex   Greenwich Village sex   Casablanca sex   Constantine sex   Rotterdam sex   rock'n'roll sex   pizza pie sex   hotdog sex   coca cola sex   peanut butter sex   cornflakes sex   buttered popcorn sex   campbell soup sex   quaker oats sex   playboy bunny funny sex   call girl many money sex   Happy Hip Happening sex   Boston beatnik bullshit sex   IBM sex   FBI sex   CIA sex   KKK sex   YMCA sex   SAS sex   KLM sex   Europe on Five sex   Voice of America sex   American Express sex   contraceptive sex   international sex   pubik pak sex   display-in-public sex   jackoff Popart sex   Hydrogen BOMB SEX, hydrogen bomb sex   hydrogen bomb sex   Bomb doom . . . no more sex!

IT IS OURS

To my angel, Olivia

Love the meaning of the love
is what I know, and feel, and think,
and plan of you
Love the reason of this poem
the images with names, symbols, sounds,
suggestions all channeled through love
Love the important action of mind and body
is that which we have to answer the whys/who/where/whats/how and
    when/
of enemies and friends
Love is our life our sun
our smiles our touch our peace our eternal gladness
it is ours love is ours

PUBIK PAK

To Andy Warhol

Good evening PUBIK PAK listners! How is the family? and especially your mother since she too has switched to PUBIK PAK? PUBIK PAK! PUBIK PAK that all-american product! PUBIK PAK displayed in store windows and on counters all over the world! PUBIK PAK the safe, the provened, the most dependable and sought out household article of its kind! PUBIK PAK fresh from your local manufactorys assembly lines has been given both seals of official approval: that of good housekeeping and the u.s. government!! why my dear listners, oriental statistics show that millions of young japanese have started using PUBIK PAK! thousands of south americans that are nonsmokers recommend PUBIK PAK! two hundred battle weary congolese mercenaries risk their lives daily for several cartons of PUBIK PAK! the nonjewish catholic mosque in egypt recommends PUBIK PAK for the aged hindu siberian church members!! senators, congressmen, and other well known garbage men are constitutionally constipated with their patriotic prefrence for PUBIK PAK! the brooklyn pitchers, brooklyn bitches and the notorious brooklyn teenage gang (the seven year itches) are destructively mad about PUBIK PAK! ten of the worlds olympic champions of boxing, skiing, seeing, peeing, screwing, chewing, running, swimming, licking, cotten picking, dicking, jumping, etc etc these top ten say that they couldnt win with out PUBIK PAK! mothers with teenage sons and fathers with teenage daughters, these parents support PUBIK PAK and they say that they wouldnt dare make it without PUBIK PAK! PUBIK PAK PUBIK PAK PUBIK PAK is . . . after all . . . in spite of . . . PUBIK PAK is . . . d i f- f e r e n t !!!!! with PUBIK PAK one can immediately feel the difference, see the difference, hear the difference, smell the difference and if one tries the new oral kit one can even taste the difference!! PUBIK PAK is great! PUBIK PAK is marvelous! PUBIK PAK is wonderful! PUBIK PAK is tremendous! PUBIK PAK is stupendous!! PUBIK PAK is . . . is . . . is magic!! the white muslims in the darkest of mississippi use integrated as well as segregated PUBIK PAK! the germans in mechanized deutschland take time off for wunderbar PUBIK PAK!! the chinese say that they wouldnt have a chinamans chance if it wasnt for PUBIK PAK!! the russians officially say that it was they that invented PUBIK PAK! the answer to world problems is PUBIK PAK! the world health organization of the united nations distributes PUBIK PAK to the poor! the norwegians, the finns, the danes and those frigid swedes even use PUBIK PAK! let me suggest the best and that is PUBIK PAK! let the goodtimes roll all night long and for gods sake dont rock or roll without PUBIK PAK! remember if you want to be popular with the girls, and with the boys you had better get hip with PUBIK PAK! noted mathematicians, atomic scientist and nuclear research technicians count on the swift rocket like speedy action of PUBIK PAK! run dont walk to your nearest dealer or legal pusher and score for PUBIK PAK!! ask for the large economical family size and save ten percent! PUBIK PAK is the answer to your personal problems! PUBIK PAK is always there to safeguard you and your loved ones! PUBIK PAK enriches your ego! PUBIK PAK energizes your action! PUBIK PAK is always ready to perform in all kinds weather conditions! for example in London a woman of royal blueblood used PUBIK PAK in a fog with her dog! PUBIK PAK is international! PUBIK PAK is strong and yet it does not rob you of that natural stimulation! PUBIK PAK will not rip or tear! PUBIK PAK has no offensive odor! PUBIK PAK does not harm delicate skin! PUBIK PAK prevents embarrassing taletell stains PUBIK PAK is recommended by spectacle wearing doctors (all over the world) PUBIK PAK is easy to handle (especially in the dark) PUBIK PAK comes in fifteen different colors and now PUBIK PAK can be had with s t r i p e s !! PUBIK PAK can be your best friend in an emergency! PUBIK PAK can be reused several times by adding the new laboratory discovery the PUBIK PAK rinse! the PUBIK PAK rinse! PUBIK PAK is the fastest selling product in the universe! spacemen, astronauts of all nations carry PUBIK PAK in their survival kits, they are always prepared for out-of-this-world chance encounters! PUBIK PAK is important! PUBIK PAK is interesting! PUBIK PAK is stimulating! PUBIK PAK is sensational! PUBIK PAK PUBIK PAK is the right way to DO IT! buy PUBIK PAK! try PUBIK PAK! cry for PUBIK PAK! buy some more PUBIK PAK apply PUBIK PAK! PUBIK PAK PUBIK PAK lay back and sigh for

PUBIK PAK!!! remember:
if it looks good
if it feels good
if it fits good
and it is good
it must be good ol' reliable P U B I K   P A K !

DONT LET THE MINUTE SPOIL THE HOUR

for the little white poem, the big painting blue, and the swinging music
   in hot red
SHE WAS HIS MUSE . . . YET REFUSED HIS HUMBLE BED
for a jug of wine (black), a few slices of cheese (yellow), and
a long lovely loaf of brown bread
for that she gave him money . . . BUT STILL REFUSED HIS BED!
for faraway trips, or making snobish social scenes, or even
in the parks holding hands (while pigeons were fed)
SHE SAID SHE DUG HIM (to hear it bugged him) 'cause she
STILL REFUSED HIS BED!!
NOW HE DONT PAINT, NOR WRITE A POEM, NOR PLAY HIS
SWINGING MUSIC IN HOT RED
BECAUSE TODAY HE IS A B E A T N I K
AND THUS THE lovesick ARTIST IS DEAD!

LATER!

To Joan

Where do they go
when they leave the love of a poet
do they go
to hell
and become flutterbyes
with rings
or do they just die
upside down
on a 19th Century rooftops!
Spare me the parting passion play
my sweet partner!
Say your sad goodbyes
to monkey ranchers!
Cast aside those tears
and old memories!
Spread your wings or legs
and take to the sky!
I'm an honest kite
so dont fly me!
Leave this soul now lazy lover!
But watch my smile
turn sneer dear!
Wave farewell at
great distance girl!
Your goodbye
must be light, fast and bitter!
Watch out woman a tear fell!
Dont wet my floor
with your bloody dry wine!
Ice on my heart for you baby!
too late to kiss my snore!
It sore of you!

Your term at this university is over!
The institute dont
need your spread anymore!
Wow how you flunked out!
You've goofed the
best test of your life!
But thanks for freeing me
for firing you!
Later baby, just never . . . later!

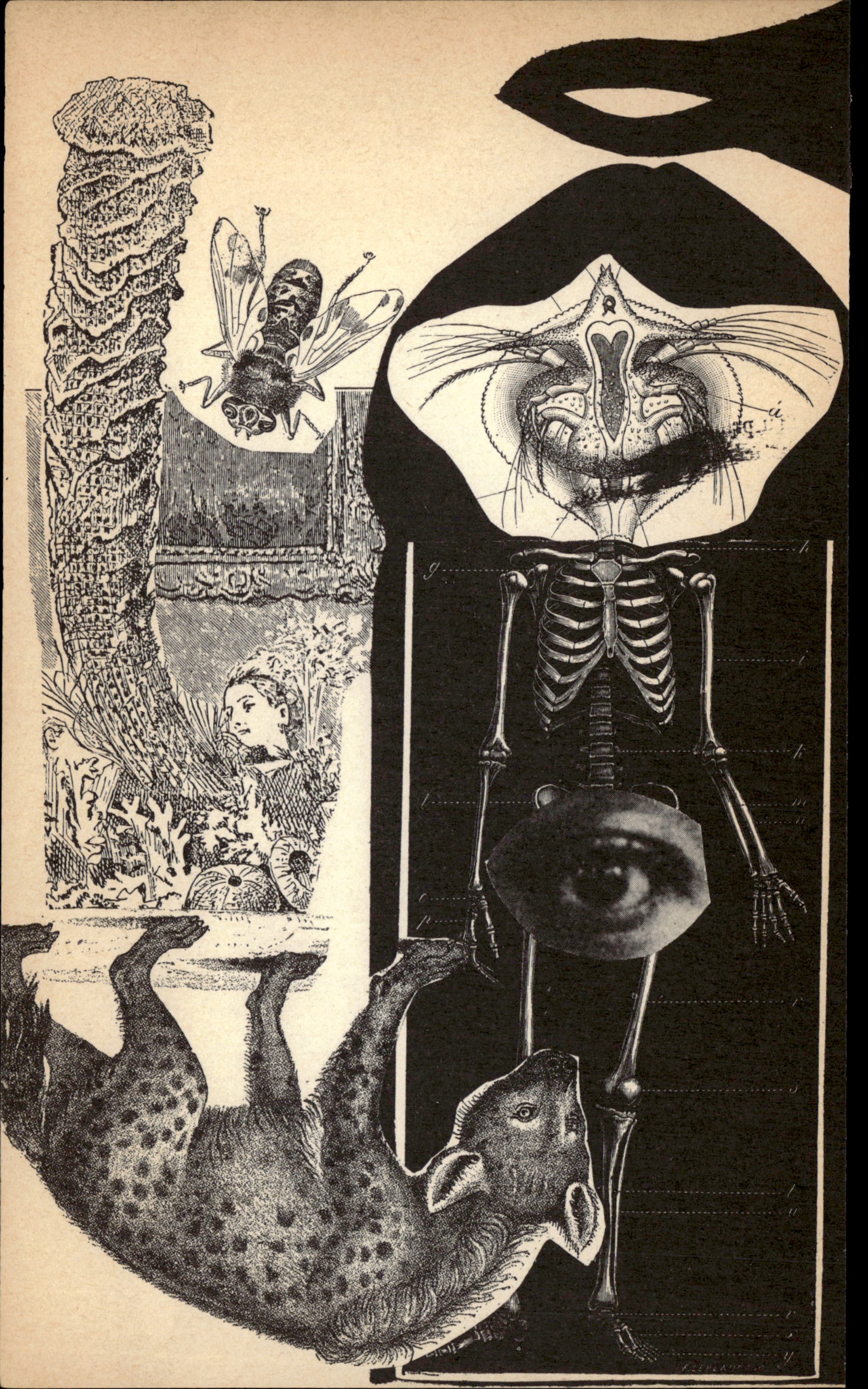

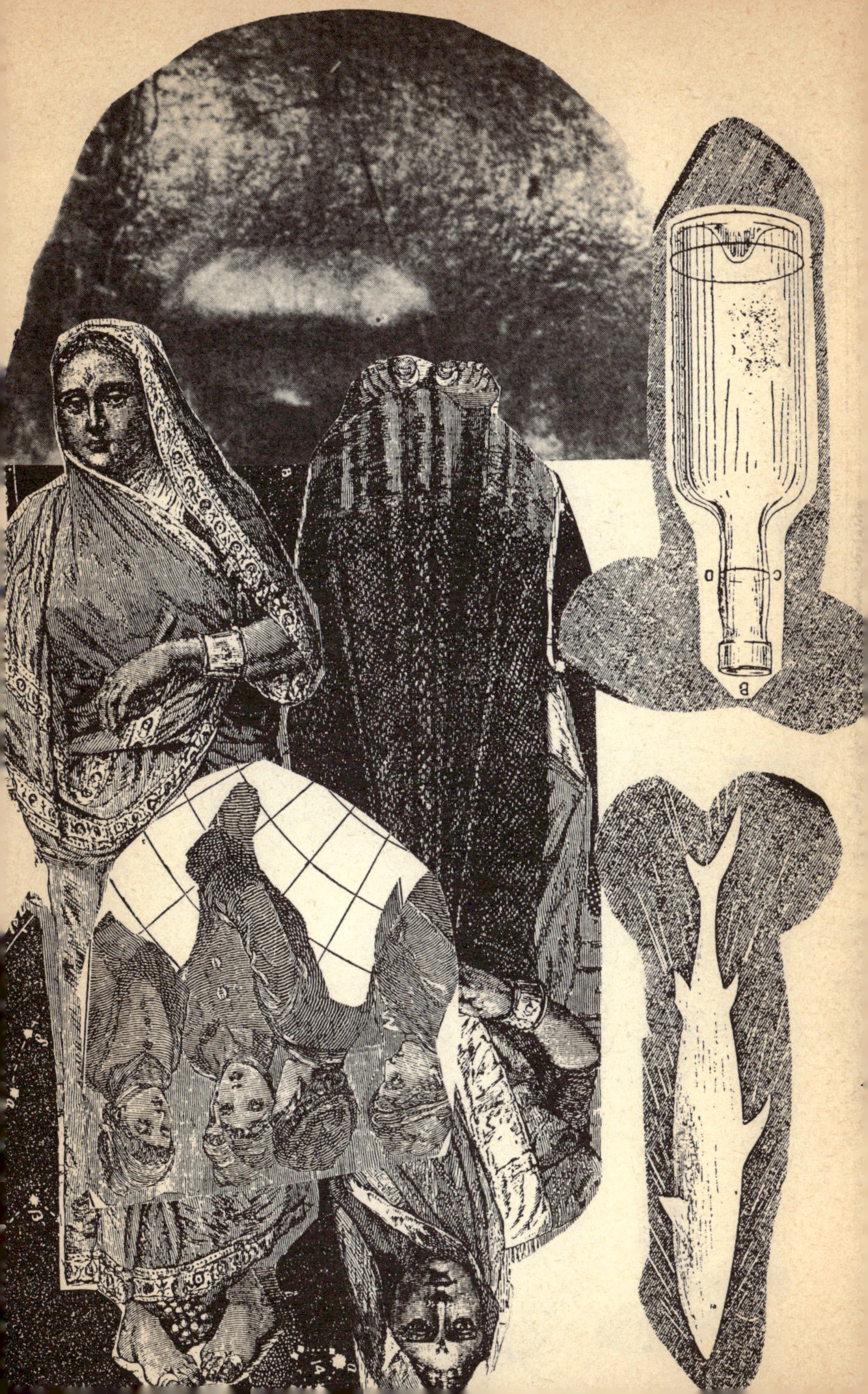

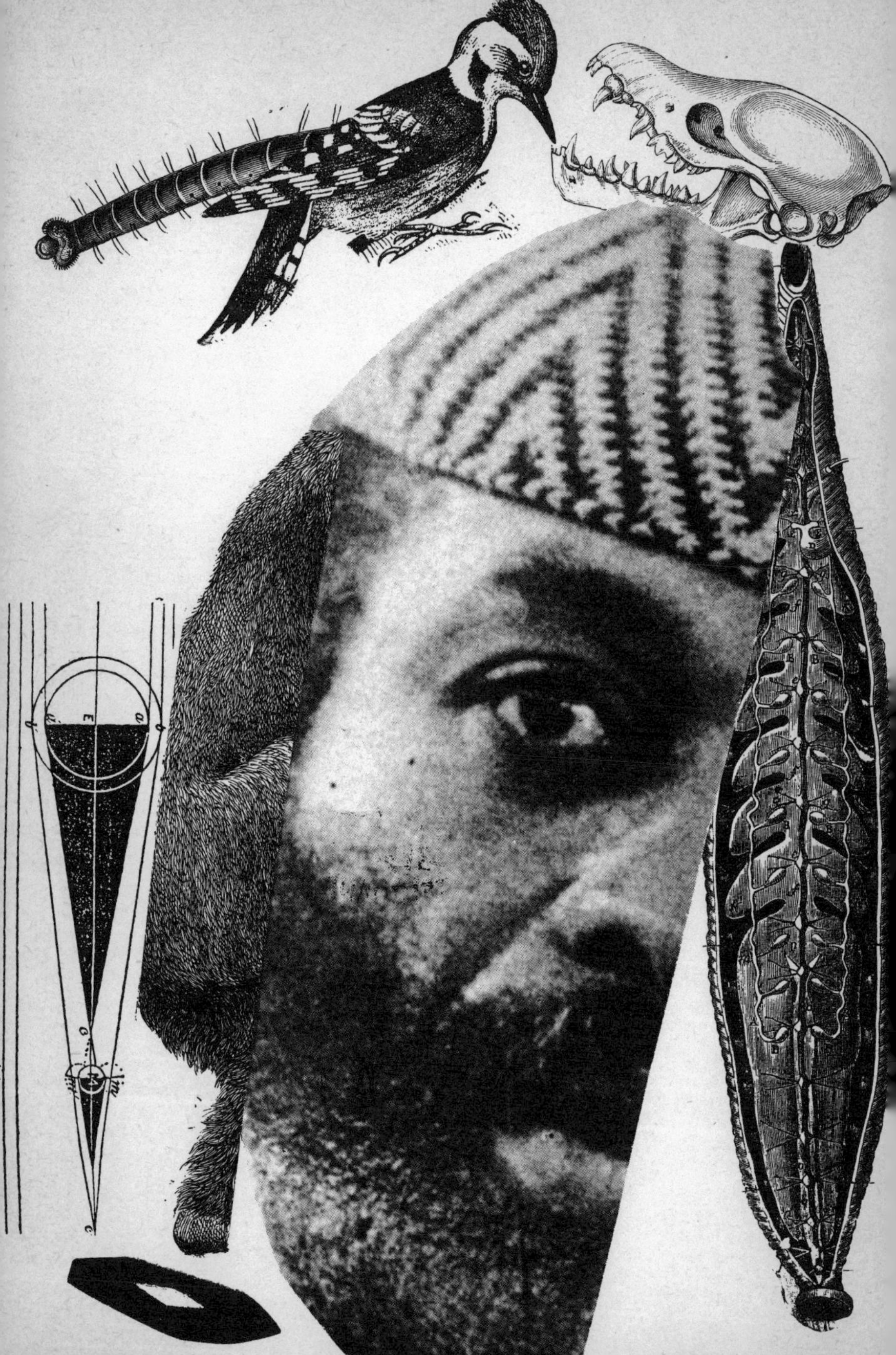

COLD PETROLEUM

she lays beside him
Her action deny him
though her emotions desire him
If she were rich
instead of a bitch
would she perhaps . . . hire him?

OVERSEA SISTER

To B. S.

when sister soul arrives on the other side
where white men lick her ass
where white boys bounce up and down on her
where white males display her as a piece of freak tail
where she dont have to pay dues they say
where she (in the beginning) has it her way
where she cashes in on the Black news of the day
where "parlez-vous-sprechen Sie" trying disguise and hide from black
    you and me
when sister soul arrives and her mind is out of shape
sister soul arrives to escape, escape, E S C A P E !

KIDSNATCHERS

To Joyce

white ones stole my babies
master pieces of humanity
white ones hide my babies
although they're black like me

ARE YOU TOO, ABLE?

Your top is more popular than your legs
your cloth often hangs
your surface is sometimes shiny/dirty/greasy/or cluttered
and yet your bottom is clean but dusty
even though some feel under you there
with their knees/and there are those that stick
large wads of chewing gum (it grows hard down there!)
between your fat or skinny/straight hard and sexless legs
Your faults are few when you are new
your patience is endless but you do turn over
you are always the object that they lay things on
your innocent look is where food awaits to be eaten
and for no fault of your own You Are Often B E A T E N !

I AM THE LOVER

To Grete

I am the lover
I sung it to your mother/sister/& daughter
I wore wooden gloves while I sung
& I just happen to have: Jacques Prévert/Jackson Pollock/&
Bessie Smith in my deep back pocket
I am the lover
I painted for you
I made collages of you
in Marrakesh/Malaga/& Malmö
I couldn't help kissing (instead of killing)
your lips/your breast/& roundass on sand dunes

I am the lover
I howled in prose
I promised a poem to (you already know who) Ornette Coleman/Albert
    Ayler/Charlie Parker/John Coltrane/all sax maniacs of colored
    races
I am the lover
I smoked pot in a plane
I gave your world another
Lumumba/Nkrumah/& Kenyatta (my sons!)
I open doors like a zipper
I am the lover
I snore in code
I pour oatmeal down tuxedo & shout: Black Balloon Biter!
Red Giraffe grabber! Cotton typewriter tickler! Ebony Eye Dropper!
Hear me! turn me onto a naked rhinoceros!
then tomorrow's newspapers will read: Monkey Ranches!
for in Paduchah/Oslo/& Timbuctu   I am the lover! !